TO PROTECT AND SERVE

TO PROTECT

A History of the San Diego Police Department and Its Chiefs

AND SERVE

1889–1989

By
Pliny Castanien

SAN DIEGO
HISTORICAL
SOCIETY

Printed in the United States of America

Published in 1993 by the San Diego Historical Society
P.O. Box 81825
San Diego, California 91238

**Publication of this book was supported by grants from the
James S. Copley Foundation and the J. W. Sefton Foundation.**

Designed by Jill Maxwell Berry, Artista Artworks
San Diego, California

Printing by Conklin Litho
San Diego, California

*The cover illustration is a photograph of Jefferson "Keno" Wilson,
Chief of the San Diego Police Department, 1909-1917.*

All photographs in this publication are from the
Photograph Collection of the San Diego Historical Society,
and the San Diego Police Officers Association.

Library of Congress Cataloging-in-Publication Data

Castanien, Pliny, 1908-
   To protect and serve : a history of the San Diego Police
Department and its chiefs, 1889-1989 / by Pliny Castanien.
      p.   cm.
   Includes bibliographical references and index.
   ISBN 0-918740-14-2 (pbk. acid-free) $14.95
   1. San Diego (Calif.).   Police Dept.—History. 2. Police–
–California—San Diego—History.   3. Police chiefs—California—San
Diego—Biography.   I . Title.
HV8148.S3C37   1993
363.2'09794'985—dc20
                                                        92-47133
                                                        CIP

The paper used in this publication meets the minimum requirements of
American National Standard for Information Sciences-Permanence of
Paper for Printed Materials, ANSI Z39.48-1984. ∞

This book is dedicated
to the men and women
of the San Diego Police Department—
yesterday, today, and tomorrow.

CONTENTS

Above: Mounted Patrolman Fred Elliott of San Diego police appears in this excellent 1908 photograph. His brother, James, was also on the force. They were sons of Deputy Sheriff Andy Elliott, pioneer lawman.

INTRODUCTION
★

In my twenty-five years as police reporter for the *San Diego Union*, a favorite assignment was to delve into the history of the force. What was to become a historical quest began when an editor asked for a story about Keno Wilson, a name which he said seemed to come up whenever people talked about the old-time cops.

Months of research were needed to do the story on Wilson. That exercise showed the poverty of the existing historical sources on the San Diego police. The years passed rapidly in the press room at police headquarters, "the cop shop," as it has come to be called by reporters. It became more and more clear to me that someone must do something, and soon, to preserve the history of the force.

After I retired in 1974, I was designated as the Police Department's historian by then–Police Chief Bill Kolender. I was given an office and the full cooperation of the department while I worked on the project. A grant for research from the Joseph Sefton Foundation proved invaluable.

What emerged is an account of a police department striving through the years to keep up with the rapid growth of a fast-moving city—a challenge that continues today.

This is the history of the San Diego Police Department for the first one hundred years, with the focus on the thirty men who were the chiefs. Some of the police chiefs were outstanding: Joe Coyne the first, Keno Wilson tall in the saddle, George Sears, Cliff Peterson, Elmer Jansen, Wes Sharp, Bill Kolender, and today Bob Burgreen.

A 1931 report of the city Civil Service Commission puts the importance of a chief in clear focus: "The success of any police department depends entirely upon the chief of police. [He must be] a man of strength and fearless character who knows the law, knows men. He must be honest, truthful, sincere, a diplomat, a disciplinarian, and have a fair amount of common sense. A man who cannot be influenced by politics, personal gain, or anything that might swerve him from his oath of office."

My aim was to inform and to draw attention to the role of the police as our first line of defense against disorder and crime. What happens when the line fails was brutally demonstrated in the Los Angeles riots of 1965 and 1992.

It is hoped that this chronicle will lead to a better understanding of the men who form that line of defense, and that the reader will finish the last page with a feeling of pride in a police department that, undermanned and often misunderstood, has performed its day-to-day tasks for more than a century, doing its best to make San Diego a better city and a safer place to live.

1

Chapter 1.
EARLY LAWMEN LOSE CONTROL

San Diegans had long dreamed of having railroad service. The community had suffered for years with slow boats to other ports and rough trips on horse-drawn stages overland to the north and east. After years of dreams and disappointment, railroad service from the city to the East Coast was inaugurated November 15, 1885. A rate war temporarily brought fares down as low as $1 from the Mississippi Valley to Southern California and touched off the biggest boom in the city's history. But the influx of transients

Frank A. T. Shaw and George W. Salladay, deputy city marshals, 1888.

eroded law and order and brought about the creation of a new city charter and a city police department.

Before the white man came to Alta California, Indian government consisted of home rule for each clan. A council of elders made important decisions and recommended punishment for law offenders. The chiefs were judge and jury. Under Spanish-Mexican regimes San Diegans were controlled by a military administration rather than by a political organization.

When San Diego became an American town with the change of flags in July 1846, new types of lawmen took over. Admission of California as a state brought the first local elections in 1850. They provided for a county sheriff, constables, a city marshal, and deputies. The town was so small the same man was elected sheriff and city marshal.

Henceforth, to the man on the street, any lawman, sheriff, constable, or marshal was always the police. This tangle in semantics exists even today, when the news media refer to deputy sheriffs as "police." But only the officers of a police department are properly police, and for a long time San Diego had no police department.

The summer after the arrival of the railroad, city officials, the press, and businessmen were complaining about the lack of law enforcement. After a wave of burglaries and robberies in August 1886, the *San Diego Union* asked this question: "What has become of the police force?"

Strictly speaking, the city didn't have one, but the newspaper continued: "The archives of the city show there is such an organization here. Yet, notwithstanding the fact the criminal element has been holding carnival during the last few days, the guardians of the peace have done nothing to indicate they are on duty." Came the November elections and the newspaper took another swipe at lawmen: "Comments of Eastern visitors who were onlookers upon the disgraceful conduct of the police force yesterday [election day] were very pronounced. They agreed in condemning the wholesale electioneering and other neglect of official duties by police [as being] most shameful. It was a disgrace to San Diego."

City Marshal Joe Coyne could hardly be criticized for electioneering, since he himself held elective office and his deputies had a personal interest in his re-election. But Coyne already was anticipating a change. A month later he announced he had ordered new badges numbered from 12 to 30 for the police. In the body of the stars were the letters, "Police of San Diego," along with the number. He also ordered police batons, handcuffs, and whistles.

It was not until two years later that San Diegans, unhappy with their local form of government, elected a board of fifteen freeholders to frame a new city charter. This provided, among other branches of government, for a police department and a chief of police—creating for the first time a municipal force to replace the city marshal system. A four-man Board of Police Commissioners to be presided over by the mayor would appoint the chief. This board could recommend matters to the Common Council (consisting of a nine-member Board of Aldermen elected at large and an eighteen-member Board of Delegates, two elected from each of nine wards). Both bodies had to approve a chief's appointment. The elected mayor had a veto but no vote.

This new charter was adopted by the city's voters on

March 2, 1889, and approved by the legislature March 16. It was effective May 16. In a city-wide election to fill the newly created posts, Douglas Gunn, former owner and editor of the *Union*, was chosen mayor.

It was apparent the great boom was fading. When the bottom finally fell out, a depression that lasted into the 1890s settled over the city. The lot of San Diego lawmen during the 1880s had not been a happy one. They had lost control of the city. Now they hoped to get it back.

Top: Eleven deputy city marshals, the entire force, posed in 1888 for this photograph, prior to formation of a city police department under a new "Freeholder's Charter" on May 16, 1889. From incorporation of San Diego as a city in 1850, city marshals and constables who proceeded the policeman were referred to as "police," which explains why the badges of these men read "police." The only one of this group to retire was Bartholomew Moriarty (standing far right). Bottom: Fifth Street, downtown San Diego in 1888.

Chapter 2.
THE LUCK OF JOE COYNE

It was no surprise when the newly created Police Board met on the evening of May 14, 1889, and appointed City Marshal Coyne to be the first police chief. The next morning the *Union* in a brief editorial commented: "The police commissioners elected 'Joe' Coyne chief for the ensuing two years. He has wide experience and a knowledge of the criminal classes possessed by few other citizens. He also has a good many enemies, who will be very hot over his appointment."

Joe Coyne, big and hearty, came to the job as the city's first chief of police with full credentials. In a portrait taken around the time of his appointment, he looks every inch a lawman—burly, a commanding presence, solemn face, Irish eyes inherited from his mother, a dark mustache above a gray Van Dyke beard, and gray hair.

He had impressed many a San Diegan during his three consecutive terms as sheriff from 1876 to 1882. A contemporary writer said this in a note attached to Coyne's capsule biography in the files of the San Diego Historical Society:

Joseph Coyne was apparently a successful and wealthy miner before he became sheriff. One would expect him to fall into the politician's role, one which was extremely popular in the early days of San Diego. It appears that most early sheriffs were more concerned with collecting taxes, selling foreclosed property, and aiming for higher positions of government than with enforcing the law.

It was not so with Coyne. He was a lawman first and foremost.

The booking logs from the 1870s repeatedly show Coyne and his chief deputy, E. W. Bushyhead, pursuing and arresting criminals throughout the county.

Our first sheriff, Agustin Haraszthy, started an Indian war by forcibly collecting taxes from native Californians. Coyne apparently knew a little more about human nature and the use of diplomacy, as is evidenced by a notice printed in the *Union* October 30, 1878: "Sheriff Coyne is now prepared to receive taxes at his office in the courthouse. It is the proud privilege of American citizenship to make yearly offering in support of our glorious government; a tastefully printed receipt is given that may be framed and hung up as a household ornament."

Coyne was a native of Cleveland, Ohio, born December 18, 1837. His father, Patrick, was a native of the same city. When Coyne was three years old, his mother, Ann Doyle Coyne, a native of Ireland, was left a widow. He came west at age fifteen.

Coyne was known as a fortunate miner but a poor businessman and an unlucky card player; he made several small fortunes and lost them all. Coyne was a miner in Northern California for fifteen years, until after the Civil War. His death certificate describes Coyne as a retired miner. He came to San Diego and was working on a road gang when gold was discovered at Julian in 1870. He and four others located and developed the famous Golden Chariot mine in Banner, east of Julian on the grade to the desert. After working it a year, he sold his interest to a partner for $50,000. With this tidy sum (equivalent in purchasing power to at least $500,000 today) he came back to San Diego and began his career as a lawman.

Coyne's personal knowledge and acquaintance with his eleven deputy marshals helped the new Board of Police Commissioners when they tackled the job of naming the first patrolmen. Candidates had to be at least five feet eight inches tall, which newspapers charged "discriminated against some veterans of the marshal's office." It was reported that one hundred applications were received for the eleven jobs.

Police salaries were averaging $80 a month for patrolmen and $100 for the one mounted officer, who was expected to provide and maintain his own horse.

The *Union* on May 30, 1889, reported that the Police Board met the night before in the office of Mayor Gunn. Long before the hour of the meeting, the hallway leading to the office was packed with a crowd of men anxious to gain fame and $80 a month.

The press was denied admittance to the meeting but did obtain a report from an "unnamed source." One by one the applicants were admitted and closely cross-examined. There were seventeen questions to be answered under oath—one on previous employment and another whether any money had been paid to secure a job with the force. Each applicant had to meet the height standard, weigh not less than 150 pounds, be not less than twenty-five nor more than fifty years of age, and at his own expense furnish a physician's certificate of good health.

There was a blank application to be filled out and signed by five citizens of good character supporting the candidate. Applicants had to be citizens of the United States and residents of San Diego for one year. At this meeting thirty-seven men were questioned, and the board adjourned until the following Friday night.

The "lucky men who will wear the star" were named at the next meeting, and again the newspapers had to obtain the story from a reliable source, as the press was still excluded. Again men crowded the hallway. Commissioners were in session for three hours before the doors were opened and a messenger left to summon Mayor Gunn and Police Chief Coyne; both arrived in a short time. Again behind closed doors, the board conferred for fully another hour. Coyne remained closeted with the board. "It is understood that the list of policemen who had been selected was given to him, in order he might see whether or not the list was perfectly satisfactory before it was given out," the *Union* reported.

Finally, at about ten o'clock, the doors again opened and the board announced the following twelve as the police officers of the city: William Penn Smith, L. P. Barton, C. J. Evert, A. M. Coates, Bartholomew Moriarty, William E. Connors, W. H. Russell Jr., J. W. Brenning, D. R. Gates, C. E. Finch, T. W. Brodnax, and George F. Dow.

Joseph Coyne, San Diego's first chief of police. He looks every inch a lawman.

who have been named most of them I know, and I think on the whole, we will have a very efficient force. I am glad of one thing. No ex-police-man has been selected who has been going around town talking about me. My intention is to name Larry Barton as my right-hand man in managing the force." Barton thus became the first assistant chief.

The Police Commission approved William Russell as clerk of the police court and of the commission, and Moriarty as city jailer. D. W. Whaley is listed in the 1889 city directory as clerk to the police chief. The chief and his men worked out of the City Hall, upstairs over the Fire Department's Engine Co. No 1, on the west side of Horton Plaza.

The collapse of the great boom left the city treasury anemic and torpedoed talk of a 25-man police department. The city simply did not have the money. Alderman George Marston moved the force be set at fifteen officers. Simon Levi seconded but added he thought twelve were enough, and in the end it was twelve men. Thus the jockeying for manpower began in 1889. It has been going on ever since.

The *Union* said the appointments created no little surprise. "Some men were selected who nobody expected would be, while others were let out who everybody supposed would be retained."

Politically, the composition of the force was eight Republicans and four Democrats. The partisan makeup of the force was a matter of concern. The elections for sheriff and city marshal were partisan in the nineteenth century, and Coyne had been the first Republican to be elected city marshal.

"Of the eight old men left out, two are Democrats and six Republicans," the newspaper reported. The "outs" were John Schneider, George W. Salladay, George H. Knowles, Walter L. Hicks, John C. White, A. F. "Fatty" Rice, John Nelson, and George W. Clark.

When reporters asked Coyne what he thought of his new force, the chief replied: "Oh, it suits me well enough. Some mighty good men have been left out, though. Of the new men

In midsummer 1889, tailor John F. Ryan's bid for uniforms was selected. New blues cost $42.50 each. This uniform was to be worn at all times while on duty, or even off duty when appearing in public, and the coat was always buttoned. An officer had to be neat and clean, have a baton or club belted around him, and present an officer-like appearance. Use of swagger sticks and umbrellas was forbidden. After some officers donned new uniforms with gold buttons, the *Union* reported people strolling the streets "are trying to get arrested for the pleasure of their company."

But the pride and pleasure of that first summer were spoiled by the kind of political interference that dogged the Police Department throughout the early years. Near the end of July the *Union* printed the following story:

The fourteen-member police force of San Diego in 1897 poses for a group photograph, with Chief James Russell, wearing cap, in center. Russell served from 1896 to 1898, and later became captain of the guard at San Quentin state prison.

A Fallen Star—A Policeman Goes to Sleep and a Star Goes to Chief Coyne

Yesterday morning Chief Coyne suspended Officer C. J. Evert who has been on duty in the southeastern part of the city. Officer Billy Connors discovered Evert asleep at his post and took his star off of him. Yesterday evening Evert came in to inform Chief Coyne that he had lost his star chasing a Chinaman. The chief had it in his possession at the time, it having been turned over to him by Connors. He knew that the story was not true and he accordingly suspended Evert pending an investigation.

A rumor went around that the suspended officer was the stool pigeon of Police Commissioner E. F. Goddard. At a board meeting Goddard denied the rumor in caustic language. The *Union* claimed its reporter was bounced from the meeting. Goddard complained about remarks the chief made to the press. The newspaper began to refer to the disagreement between Goddard and Coyne as an "imbroglio." Coyne in an interview said if they wanted to investigate his office, they could do so. He said he had lived in San Diego too long to be "downed by persons who are now making charges against me in the street and on the corners."

The *Union* on August 7, 1889, printed this editorial:

The commotion in police circles is a tempest in a teapot and harmful to San Diego. The Police Commission, when they assumed their places under the charter, made probationary appointments to the police force. The term of appointment was for approximately 60 days. At the end of that period, whether wisely or not, they dispensed with the services of several policemen and appointed others to take the places made vacant.

Since the action was taken, the street corners have been alive with rumors, and much of it has appeared in the press of the city, all of which is unnecessary, if not possibly wrong. We are ready to endorse and foster any action taken in the direction of honest city government. This the people want and this the people will have, cost what it may.

On the other hand, we are unreservedly opposed to public officers being condemned without investigation by the proper board which represents the best elements of the city. And certainly after investigation, if an officer is continued in service and in place, the criticism should apply to the board and not to the individual continued in office by the board. This appears to be the situation, so far as Chief Coyne is concerned.

Commissioner Goddard is wrong, and doing an injustice to the board of which he is a member. When the board investigated police affairs and dismissed five officers and continued the chief, that should have been the end of it.

His [Coyne's] life for years in this city must stand for something, whatever may have been his political mistakes. He is certainly entitled to proper endorsement up to this time. The efforts of Commissioner Goddard to discredit Mr. Coyne should apply, by all means, to the board of which he is a member. This is right according to the rules of fair play.

The newspaper's complaints about closed meetings produced results. The *Union* on August 16 reported that the Police Board convened the night before in its first open session since taking office. Chief Coyne made a report of the force's activities from May 12 to August 12. Coyne said he had only nine officers to cover the large area of the city, and considering this small force, breaking in new men, and lack of supervision, the officers worked in harmony and hoped to keep crime low.

Then Coyne got down to brass tacks and took his gloves off:

I would suggest to your honorable board that officers be requested to report to this office all official acts, and that they receive all orders pertaining to the discharge of their duties from this [Coyne's] office, thereby avoiding unpleasant difficulties.

In conclusion, let me ask your honorable body that in the future when charges are preferred against me by your honorable committee, that I be notified in due form and not arraigned on the street corners and cars. I would also prefer being tried by your honorable body rather than though the press, as I have been compelled to do lately in order to vindicate myself before the public.

At this point Goddard and another board member attacked Coyne for comments he had made in the press; Mayor Gunn left the chair; Commissioner E. W. Bushyhead assumed temporary chairmanship and moved the matter be tabled. Things had been getting out of hand for a public meeting. After a general discussion among commissioners, Goddard calmed down. Motions were made left and right and the board was in and out of order until finally it adopted Bushyhead's motion to table the discussion. On August 27 the *Union* put the imbroglio to rest: "HARMONY PREVAILS ONCE MORE." Mayor Gunn said he believed the chief to be a faithful and honest worker.

But there was continuing concern that the city might be spending more than it could afford on city government, including the newly organized police force.

In his annual report for 1889 (January to May) made to the Common Council May 25, Mayor Gunn said his main task had been to put into operation an entirely new municipal government, new not only to San Diego but to California. This new charter, he explained, was similar to systems in other states. To critics who complained the new system was more expensive, Gunn replied it was less expensive because there were twenty-seven fewer city employees, giving the city a saving of $2,223 per month. The mayor said the Police Department had maintained public order with the smallest force employed by any city of 30,000.

Any reduction of the force was opposed by the Police Board. The original report of this worthy board, adopted September 23, 1889, survives. They reached this conclusion:

To what extent can the police force be reduced? We answer it ought not be reduced at all. We hold citizens have the right to demand protection for their lives and property even while the city is in a profound state of peacefulness.

To what extent should the maintenance of the police force be left to a constabulary? We answer we deem it a dangerous experiment to leave this city at the mercy of men whose only incentive to action is the pecuniary gain arising from arrests, summoning of witnesses, attendance at court, etc.

We believe maintenance of peace and enforcement of the municipal and criminal laws should be left to no set of men who are not responsible directly to the city authorities, whose character has not been examined into and found to be irreproachable, and who for pecuniary gain might be tempted to persecute innocent men.

The experience which our city has had with appointees whose fees are dependent upon the extent of their official acts should be a warning for all time to come. To the question, to what extent special policemen may be appointed for service in the outlying districts, where no protection whatever is now offered by city authority, we would say that special policemen may be appointed anywhere on application to the chief of police, if paid by the applicants.

But in that same month, the Board of Delegates passed a resolution: "Because of the profound state of peacefulness in the city it is the consensus of the board the present police force is far in excess of requirements of the city for preservation of order."

The strength of the Police Department was duly cut back.

On September 30, 1889, just four months after formation of the metropolitan police force, Chief Coyne submitted a report to the Police Board. The original of this report is in the files of the San Diego Historical Society. By this time the chief had acquired proper stationery for his office, and on one of these letterheads he wrote in longhand:

List of Police officers showing beats and place of duty to take effect October 1, 1889, at 12 o'clock noon—also number of star worn by each officer.

Officer Russell #9, police court, day; Officer Moriarty #4, City Jail, day; Officer White #1, city mounted, night; Officer Gates #12, Fourth Street and west, G Street and north, day; Officer Coates #5, Sixth Street and east, day; Officer McCarthy #8, Sixth Street and east, H (Market) Street and south. night; Officer Brenning #10, Fifth Street, day; Officer Brodnax #11, Fourth Street and west, H Street and south, night; Officer Alroid #6, Sixth Street and east, G Street and north, night; Officer Starbird #3, Fifth Street, night; and Officer Hickey, #2, Fourth Street and west, H Street and south, day.

Coyne in his first yearly report said the large number of dogs roaming city streets had become a serious nuisance. He asked city fathers to impose a dog tax, which they did. The chief said there was need for some improvement in the City Jail and some provision should be made for the

Police Chief Coyne, asked if he approved of the selection of the first city policemen, said it suited him well enough, adding "my intention is to name Larry Barton as my right hand man." Barton, at left, thus became the first assistant police chief. Bartholomew Moriarty, a deputy city marshal in 1888 was one of the original city officers chosen in 1889. He served as first jailer, bailiff to the city court, and then as first captain.

accommodation of female prisoners; and better facilities were needed for the temporary care of sick persons picked up on the streets. All this would cost money.

"I am certainly not an advocate of extravagance in public expenditure," Chief Coyne wrote, "but I cannot believe there is any real economy in depriving the citizens of this city of a reasonable degree of police protection, because during the past two or three years we have been favored by a singular immunity from serious crimes. We have no guaranty of perpetual immunity. The very presence of an adequate force acts as a check upon the criminal class, and affords a sense of safety to the citizens. Our police and fire departments ought to be kept upon a reasonable standard of efficiency."

And not everyone in the city thought there were too many cops. Two wards, Coronado Beach and Old Town, each asked for a policeman. The 1889 charter had extended the city's boundaries to include Coronado and North Island and all of the bay, thereby expanding the city's area in square miles from twelve to seventy-eight. For a time, the city struggled along with less than ten policemen. Coronadans objected to paying taxes to the city of San Diego and launched a campaign to form their own city. This may have been instrumental in persuading the city of San Diego to add patrolmen.

The Police Board in February 1890 asked and received authority to appoint two additional officers. At that time the police commissioners said, "The entire command of the Police Department is now complete, including a jailer, and the cost is less than 43 cents per capita." (San Francisco paid $1.56 and Los Angeles $1.60.)

But the good people of Coronado were not persuaded. Their incorporation drive succeeded in an 1891 election.

Lady Luck was to jilt the well-liked Irishman Coyne, starting with the failure of the police commissioners to reappoint him at the end of his two-year term as chief. In April 1891, the press reported the commissioners met the night before and elected as chief William H. Crawford, age forty-four. The vote: Crawford 3; Coyne 1; Worthing 1.

Coyne served as a deputy under Sheriff Ben Hill in 1893. Then the county Board of Supervisors appointed him night watchman at the courthouse. His Banner mine fortune had been dissipated through the years. Coyne's name last appeared in the city directory of 1894. He moved to San Francisco with his family where, after a three-year illness, he had a heart attack and died February 5, 1916. He was 78.

Newspaper obituaries mourned his death and remembered him as an efficient, good lawman. But when his luck ran out and he fell to the most menial of peacekeeping jobs at the courthouse, it was enough to break a stout heart.

Late in 1989 as the department was celebrating its one hundredth anniversary, a family member revealed that the great-granddaughter of Chief Coyne, Laura McGowan, twenty-nine, was a street cop working out of the Western Division. She joined the force on April 24, 1986, and was a member of the 107th academy class.

One wonders what would be Joe's reaction if he knew Laura, a woman, is carrying on his tradition as a street cop. The best guess is he would be surprised but proud.

Chapter 3.
THE REVOLVING DOOR: 1891-1909

W. H. Crawford held the office of chief of police only three months. To understand his misfortune, it is necessary to look at some practices before and during his term of office. In the 1880s San Diego was a wide-open town. Gambling, liquor, and prostitution flourished, all in spite of the better elements' knowledge of this condition in Stingaree Town, the city's equivalent of San Francisco's Barbary Coast. The infamous Stingaree, known to merchant mariners and Navy sailors alike, was found south of Market Street (then called H Street) in a neighborhood of Chinese gambling halls, saloons, bawdy houses, and cribs.

All this was cheerfully accepted by most of the citizenry as essential to the economy of a thriving seaport. But there were many complaints about the constabulary. This was one citizen's plaintive protest in a newspaper: "It is all very well to suppress hoodlumism, but what seems to be urgently needed is some authority to suppress the constables."

There were rumors that the officers were prone to shoot without regard for the safety of bystanders. There was talk of unemployed lawmen who resorted to questionable practices to support themselves, family, and horse. Herbert C. Hensley in his *Memoirs* tells the lament of a disgusted departing visitor to an editor: "I would rather live in peace and security in the fitful climate of the East than to have a bullet accidentally lodged in my body when walking out to enjoy the balmy air of the Pacific in San Diego."

And Crawford's misfortune is worth recording in some detail because it involves this very issue, still of major concern to citizens today—that is, the use or misuse of deadly force by persons acting under the color of the law.

The appointment of Crawford seemed auspicious. The *San Diego Sun* and the *Union* both referred to him as "Captain" Crawford, a title he earned on the Chicago Police Department. The *Sun* on May 28, 1891, said Crawford had experience going back to 1874. He resigned as a Chicago deputy sheriff when he came to the Pacific Coast. In San Diego he had held the job of deputy U. S. marshal, working out of the office in Los Angeles, a job he resigned to become chief.

The brief record left in newspapers shows him to have been a sincere lawman who knew how to better employee relations. Press accounts indicate he had fourteen men. He advocated and obtained for them a one-week vacation every year, and a day off each week. Officers had been working seven days a week for two years.

And there was nothing that early summer to warn of the impending tempest that bore down on Crawford when the USS *Charleston* sailed into the harbor on July 4, 1891. The crew was warmly welcomed. The cruiser had been at sea for several months chasing the ship *Itita*, believed to be running contraband guns to South America. Sailors were overdue shore leave and headed straight for the Stingaree when they got it.

Sometime earlier, U. S. Marshal George E. Gard of Los Angeles, who was Crawford's former boss and who had jurisdiction over federal affairs here, had authorized C. W. Breedlove, a hanger-on around the police station, to round up seven sailors absent without leave from the revenue cutter *Ranger*.

When a delegated officer of the U. S. marshal returned a sailor to his ship at the request of the commanding officer, it was customary that a $10 reward be paid and then be deducted from the bluejacket's pay. This proved to be a big incentive for unemployed lawmen, because $10 was really $10 in those days.

Breedlove, the man designated as a deputy U. S. marshal, had been recommended by several lawmen. Breedlove was in the military register for San Diego in 1884 as a deputy city marshal. He had carried out his duty of returning the AWOL *Ranger* sailors without incident.

When Marshal Gard sent Chief Crawford descriptions of eleven men out of 115 of the port watch who had failed to report back to the *Charleston*, the chief asked the mayor for instructions. The mayor told him, "Do nothing."

So it is reasonable to assume that Chief Crawford turned over to Breedlove the list of AWOL sailors from the *Charleston*, although the record does not clearly show who gave Breedlove the list. In any case, Crawford did not deputize Breedlove.

Breedlove lost no time in enlisting the aid of W. W. Webb, a burly man with some police experience, to give him a hand in the roundup. They took a run into the Stingaree armed with billy clubs and six-shooters and soon found four of the AWOL sailors in a saloon.

9

A group of officers posing while on a police detail in the early 1900s. The man wearing civilian clothing, Derby hat and holding a baton, is Harvey F. Shepherd, who joined the department August 4, 1909, made sergeant in 1912 and lieutenant in 1913.

recruited in the Court Exchange bar for $2.50 an hour, Breedlove to foot the bill.

Word spread downtown of more trouble pending between the marshals and sailors in Stingaree Town, and spectators numbered about forty when the pitched battle did occur.

Newspaper accounts said witnesses sided with the sailors, and one saloonkeeper actually knocked Mendenhall down with a blow of his fist. The "posse" all wore civilian clothing, and sailors later testified they were not shown any badges. The fighting started in the street and was resumed nearby in Pete Cassidy's saloon, The Eclipse, where a handcuffed sailor was rescued when other shipmates, one armed with pipe, bowled over the "marshals." Both "possemen" and sailors took a beating.

The brawl started at noon and was over in half an hour. Score: Breedlove 0; Sailors 0. Total returned to ship in two days by Breedlove and party: three, for $30.

It was all over, except for one fatal detail. One sailor, Joseph W. Brown, about twenty-five, a fireman second class from Vallejo, had taken a heavy club blow in the temporal area. He staggered into the Kansas Stables at Fourth and J streets. A stable boy thought Brown was drunk. They bedded him down in a grain bin to sleep it off. At 1:45 p. m. the boy told the office the sailor was mighty still and had blood on his face.

Joey Brown, as he was known to shipmates, was dead from frontal skull fractures, the result of the blow he received in the fight. He was one of the *Charleston's* AWOL sailors. Coroner M. B. Keller was summoned, the body removed to the San Diego Undertaking Parlor, and an autopsy ordered. A call went out for witnesses to testify at the inquest. The captain of the *Charleston* was notified, by none other than Breedlove, who returned to town with the ship's surgeon and took the doctor to see the body.

The next morning the *Union's* banner headline thundered "Clubbed to Death" in top position, with the rest of the head reading: "Bloody Encounter in Stingaree Town. Deputy United States Marshals Exceed Their Authority. An Indignant Populace. Threats of Lynching. Breedlove Gives Himself Up."

When told they were under arrest, the bluejackets didn't follow the book. They resisted, even after Breedlove bawled out he was a deputy U. S. marshal. Being an experienced hand and figuring two against four was poor odds, Breedlove retreated uptown with Webb to get help. This was Monday, July 13, 1891.

The original four sailors went back to their ship, each saving ten bucks. On Tuesday, Breedlove heard eight or ten AWOL sailors were still ashore. He and Webb found two in a Fifth Street saloon between I and J Streets. These sailors also resisted and a lively fight broke out. Witnesses said Breedlove and Webb used their billies freely.

Half a dozen other sailors joined the combat, and again Breedlove and Webb were forced to retreat, both sides being exhausted. Clubs, handcuffs, and a couple of revolvers used by the bounty hunters had been seized by the sailors. Bluejackets, flushed with victory over the law, retired to the Silver Moon saloon at Third and I streets and, regrouping on the second floor, took stock of wounds. One had taken a club blow above one eye, a serious injury. The others only had bruises. Alcohol helped soothe the aches and pains. Some sailors went directly back to ship, not wanting more trouble.

Breedlove, highly displeased with the mauling he had received, went uptown to form his own "posse," which finally consisted of Webb, Tell Grether, Peter Gurrie, Charles Wilson, Dan Mendenhall and A. M. Coates. All were big men who knew how to use their fists and clubs. They were

10

The story ran through three columns of hand-set type. The *Union* editorial summed it up. The editors were unable to recall any other infraction of peace in the history of the city which had so aroused citizens to white heat and explosive indignation. The words "abominable, murderous, dastardly, unnecessary" were used to characterize the conduct of the deputy marshals. The *Union* said the order to return sailors to their ship did not read "dead or alive," and the affair illustrated the danger of delegating authority and power to enforce it to irresponsible persons, to whom a paltry reward was to be gained at the expense of human blood. "It is to the everlasting credit of our own peace officers [police] that they were not implicated, but that the offenders are deputy United States marshals."

Despite the assurance of the editorial writers, big trouble was ahead for Police Chief Crawford. The *Union's* 1889 warning against bounty hunters should have been remembered and heeded. Even though they had been acting under the color of federal authority, the members of the "posse" were held to answer to local law enforcement officers. Breedlove and Wilson were arrested on the district attorney's charges of murder, and others of the "posse" for assault with deadly weapons. All were in the County Jail by nightfall except Mendenhall, who later surrendered. The jail was an armed camp of deputy sheriffs, as word spread of a possible roping party.

The coroner's inquest, preliminary hearing, and Superior Court trial established that Chief Crawford was at the scene of the fatal clubbing. He testified he was there in a buggy but saw no fighting. Testimony was heard that after the first resistance by *Charleston* sailors the police chief gave Breedlove four billy clubs. Crawford on the stand said he didn't think much of U. S. Marshal Gard and thought Gard treated him and Breedlove "unfairly."

Breedlove's trial dragged on into the next year. Wilson was found innocent. A motion was entered for dismissal of criminal cases against all the others except Breedlove. Breedlove remained free, but he died of thirst and exposure in the desert the next summer while on a trip to the Baja California gold mines, according to Hensley's *Memoirs*.

Although Chief Crawford contended he was not responsible for the actions of federal officials and persons authorized by them to act as bounty hunters, there was no public inclination to let the chief off the hook. Crawford's case was disposed of without delay. At a Police Board meeting July 29, 1891, the mayor had the clerk read Crawford's resignation, effective September 1. It was accepted immediately. San Diego had always been a good liberty port for sailors and it did not want to get the reputation of being a dangerous and unfriendly town.

It was not to be the last time that charges of brutality and excessive use of force embarrassed a San Diego police chief.

An immediate vote was taken for a new police chief. W. H. Pringle was elected by four votes, to one for G. C. Arnold. Pringle, well known in the city and county, was the owner of a large ranch and other properties and was reputed to be worth $100,000. But it appeared no one had consulted Mr. Pringle about running the police force. On August 25 the clerk of the police board read a message in which Pringle thanked the commission for the honor but declined to serve, giving as his reason the pressure of private business. Perhaps he had his doubts about job security.

The mayor commented, "Gentlemen, as Mr. Pringle has never qualified, the office of chief of police will be vacant." Yet, by a quirk of history, W. H. Pringle has always been listed as the third chief of police, and we do not intend to depart from that tradition.

Commissioner Goddard then placed in nomination Jacob Brenning, the officer on the Fifth Street beat. The vote was unanimous for him, and everyone, including the press, was pleased. "It was a wise and commendable move, not only because it promoted a man from the ranks, a precedent which might hereafter be followed without deviation," the *Union* said. It wasn't, until much later.

The afternoon Brenning was elected, a *Union* reporter found him walking his beat. Thus he learned who was the new chief, to his total surprise.

Brenning's term began August 28, 1891. He was forty-two. A native of Nova Scotia, he stood six feet one inch tall; had a dark complexion, blue eyes, and black hair; and had a stub finger on his left hand. Like Joe Coyne, he looked every inch a lawman.

Chief Brenning had only seven officers under his command when he took office, but there was a civic move to give him an adequate force to look after the waterfront. Under Jake Brenning, the strength of the force and also the wages and working conditions of San Diego police officers improved. Still, manpower continued to go up and down like a yo-yo, causing headaches for those trying to schedule patrols. The number of officers increased or decreased as the economy demanded. The force was increased by three additional policemen in the spring of 1892, and George F. Dow, W. L. Warner, and John M. McInnis were sworn in. McInnis later became sergeant. This increased total strength to eleven officers and the chief.

City Ordinance No. 222, adopted in July of 1893, set the salary of the chief at $125 monthly; that of mounted patrolmen at $115 each; and that of patrolmen at $100 each. It set the strength at ten officers—two mounted and eight on foot, with one of the patrolmen to be detailed as jailer. This was fewer men than when the department was established, but at the end of 1893 the commissioners increased the strength from ten to fifteen.

Police commissioners did some tinkering in 1895, increasing the chief's salary to $150 a month and reducing vacation time. Officers' salaries and hours were trimmed.

As 1897 dawned, there were fourteen policemen for a city of 22,000. A generous pat on the back was given police when the mayor released reports for the year. Police Judge Thomas

Hayes wrote that "San Diego can be proud of herself on having a most excellent police force; all are men of honor, courage, and respectability." The department would undoubtedly have preferred that the city fathers were as generous with their dollars as they were with praise.

It is apparent that Jake Brenning carried on the traditions of Coyne in his fearlessness and dedication to his job. His administration of six years was one of stability. An ebony baton survives, with a gold cap engraved "Xmas, 1895"; the gold leaf on the handle bears the engraving "To Chief of Police J. W. Brenning. From his friends, San Diego, Calif."

Left: James Russell, fifth chief of police. Right: Jóse Cota, the first Hispanic police officer in San Diego, appointed 1897.

Jake Brenning served well, was popular with his fellow officers and citizens, and was chief most of the Gay Nineties, until May 9, 1897, when he resigned. Newspapers said he held an extensive mining interest at Banning at the time of his retirement.

Sergeant John M. McInnis served as acting chief for a few days. The police commissioners acted quickly and wisely to select a new chief, James Russell, who was elected May 4, 1897. The next day Russell posted a $10,000 bond and asked for a couple of days to settle personal affairs.

"Comment on the street yesterday in regard to Mr. Russell was generally favorable," the *Union* reported. "He is conceded to possess first-rate ability as a detective and executive officer."

Russell, a native of New York City, was forty-four when he took office. He came with his parents to California in 1859 at the age of six. They first lived in San Francisco and soon moved to Stockton, where he received his education. Jim came to San Diego when he was seventeen, a move made because his mother's health demanded a more gentle climate. From 1870 until he became chief he had been a continuous resident of San Diego.

In those twenty-seven years he became widely acquainted with Southern and Lower California, and he made his mark as a lawman. He became a deputy under City Marshal Capt. A. P. Knowles in 1874. Later he was elected constable several times and also served as a deputy sheriff and deputy U. S. marshal. A Republican, he was a strong fighter for the party and was the G.O.P. candidate for sheriff in 1888, losing to the Democratic incumbent, Edward Bushyhead.

For thirteen years before becoming chief, Russell had

managed a detective and patrol service in the business area, functioning as an auxiliary to the police and an aid to law enforcement.

After making the customary "work in harmony with the force" statements to the press, Russell settled into his new job. Sgt. McInnis, the interim acting chief, who said he could not work "in harmony" with Russell, resigned. Officer Joe Cota, another former constable and all-around lawman, was appointed sergeant to replace McInnis. The one sergeant of the force was the second man in charge, taking over if the chief was unable to work or was absent.

Russell's first major move was to change hours. For himself, he set "from 7 a.m. to any time at night that business makes it necessary for me to be on hand—from 12 to 18 hours daily." The new patrol shifts, which have remained in effect to the present day, were from 7 a.m. to 3 p.m., 3 p.m. to 11 p.m., and 11 p.m. to 7 a.m. The new shifts gave the officers a chance to use streetcars on all shifts, saving them the expense of hiring or keeping a horse or buggy.

The new chief successfully opposed cutting the pay of officers and sought to increase manpower. In his report for 1897—half a dozen pages filed early in 1898 and for the first time typewritten—Russell said he needed more men, no less than three and eight if possible. He warned that the existing force would be totally inadequate in the event of a riot. He advocated appointing two detectives. The department needed a fund to check out criminals and to investigate crimes. He suggested installing patrol and signal systems so officers on beats could keep in touch with headquarters, and urged the city to provide a patrol wagon.

"We have a large harbor and have never used harbor police," Russell said, adding at all times there should be at least two men on the harbor beat. He stressed the need for a larger police station. Most of Chief Russell's suggestions for expansion and improvement were ignored by the city fathers for years and then were put into effect under his successors.

War fever ran high in San Diego in the spring of 1898 after the battleship USS *Maine* blew up in the harbor at Havana, Cuba. Only a few months earlier the Navy had begun to take measures to fortify the San Diego harbor, and as news reached the city of the beginning of the Spanish-American War, the first warship was based here. "Minute Men" rallied around the flag and a national guard unit was recruited. All

Above: Police Chief Edward W. Bushyhead. Right: Bushyhead (seated in center) with his officers in front of City Hall which housed the police station. Seated on the left is Capt. Bartholomew Moriarty and on the right is Thomas W. Brodnax, a sergeant who later became sheriff.

this was coordinated with police, and patrolmen handled the traffic caused by a patriotic parade just two days before the declaration of war in April 1898.

For police and all hastily formed military units who were placed on alert for Spanish invaders, the war was over almost before it began, ending on August 12, 1898. It was the first war to cause alarm in San Diego's harbor, but not the last.

Russell made one major mistake as police chief—he dabbled in politics. In the mayoral election of 1899 he bet on the wrong person. He opposed Edwin M. Capps, who won the mayor's race, and the end of Russell's career as chief was in sight. Charles S. Hardy, a political power and new police commissioner, wanted Russell's scalp. He proposed E. W. Bushyhead, the Democrat who had defeated Russell for sheriff in 1888, to be chief.

On May 5, Judge N. R. Conklin, also a member of the Police Commission, in a letter to Russell indicated he supported Mayor Capps but did it with regret "as I recognize you have been the best chief the city of San Diego has ever had." Even Mayor Capps said he found no fault with the chief's administration.

So at the next meeting of police commissioners it was only a formality to elect a chief for the next two years. The vote to name Bushyhead was unanimous. Commissioner Eugene Daney paid tribute to Chief Russell, regretting he could not be retained. But Russell was out on May 9, 1899.

When a commissioner asked the mayor when Bushyhead would take office, the reply was "Right away."

Edward Wilkerson (Ned) Bushyhead, who had helped found the *San Diego Union*, was sixty-seven years old when he became police chief in 1899. A journalist turned lawman, he set type for the first newspaper published in the Indian Territory prior to Oklahoma's statehood. One of his grandfathers was a Cherokee. As a lad of seven he made the famous march of the Cherokees from Tennessee to Indian Territory. He came overland to California in 1850, was a miner in the northern counties three years and, after meeting the fiery Illinois attorney Jeff Gatewood in Calaveras County, became foreman of Gatewood's newspaper plant.

Bushyhead in 1868 brought the printing plant to San Diego for Gatewood, and was his foreman-printer for eight months. With C.P. Taggart he bought the plant and weekly newspaper. He then outlasted four partners and had an interest when the *Union* became a daily. He sold his interest in 1873 for $5,000 and took a long trip back East. On his return he became a deputy sheriff in 1875 and held the position until he was elected sheriff in the fall of 1882, succeeding Joe Coyne. He served two terms as sheriff and retired to become a partner in a printing business. Bushyhead was a member of the Police Commission that named Coyne the first chief in 1889.

Bushyhead met Russell on the afternoon of May 15, 1899, in the police chief's office and took possession, posting a

Above: Officers J. C. Schultz, Corporals S.D. Mullinix and M.R. Zimmerman, Kirkland, Doty, Demsy, Sgt. Edward F. Forbes, and Henry Churchman in 1903. Below: Police Chief Albert A. Thomas.

$10,000 bond. Police Sgt. C. L. Farwell, who joined the force on January 14, 1903, recalled in an interview in the *Evening Tribune* in 1930 that the department had fourteen officers, including the chief, and that Chief Bushyhead and his "finest" sported mustaches and helmets.

In his 1899 annual report Chief Bushyhead recommended setting aside not more than $25 or $30 a month to be used as a "Secret Service fund," as certain work was almost impossible for uniformed officers and required hiring persons outside the force. The department still did not have a detective.

In May 1900 the city authorized purchase of a bicycle for use by police—the coming of a bicycle patrol. The years before the turn of the century had been difficult years for the city's economy, but the construction of small homes and cottages continued, overflowing the mesas above the downtown district and adding to the problems of the police. Bicycles would help.

By this time a new City Hall had been built, at Fifth and G streets. The police moved in. Bushyhead had an office on the second floor, and the police station was on the ground floor with a G Street entrance. The locker room and gym were in the basement.

Ned Bushyhead was known as a quiet man and stayed true to character as chief. His 1901 report was headlined in the *Union:* "SAN DIEGO IS A MORAL, HEALTHY CITY. 614 arrests, over half of which were drunks, 441 convicted." Bushyhead had fourteen patrolmen that year, with Tom Brodnax second in command as a mounted sergeant. In 1903 newspapers praised Bushyhead for his four years as chief, saying he had brought the department to a high state of efficiency.

Bushyhead was seventy years old as he approached reappointment time. He wanted to stay on the job but was getting tired. This had some bearing on the action reported May 5, 1903, under a *Union* headline: "CHIEF BUSHYHEAD IS SUPPLANTED." Albert A. Thomas was the Police Board's selection as the new police chief. Bushyhead died in Alpine in 1907, two days after his seventy-fifth birthday, and is buried in the family plot in Tahlequah, Oklahoma.

Thomas was a native of Springfield, Illinois. During the Civil War he served in Tennessee with the 44th Iowa Infantry. After the war he returned to farm pursuits, marrying in 1867 and two years later moving to Nebraska. In the fall of 1879 he was elected sheriff there, serving until 1881. He came to San Diego in April 1887 and as a real estate salesman suffered heavy losses a year later in the land bust. Then he worked in San Diego as a conductor for the street railway and as a part-time officer at the U. S. Customs office at the San Ysidro border crossing.

Left: George W. Moulton, who served less than three months and later, as county assessor, had the dubious distinction of being sent to state prison. Right: Chief William T. Neely.

Thomas served two terms (1903–1907) as police chief, being appointed the second time after John L. Sehon became mayor. This was a serene period, marred only by the tragic explosion on July 21, 1905, of the boilers of the gunboat USS *Bennington* while it was moored in the harbor. The blast killed sixty-six men.

There was an important sign of the times during Thomas' second term: the first vehicle license was issued for an automobile. The city began to take on the appearance of a substantial municipality. In 1904 the council set the yearly salary of patrolmen at $1,000, mounted officers at $1,180. In his 1905 report, Thomas said the department needed officers to patrol in Point Loma, Pacific Beach, and La Jolla, which were growing fast. He wanted two more mounted officers and four foot patrolmen.

When John F. Forward won the mayor's office in 1907, a new police chief was in order. Forward's administration was generally regarded as a good one, but his first choice of a police chief was unfortunate. George W. Moulton, a Spanish-American War veteran and Fallbrook newspaper publisher, was not a legal resident of the city and could not take office as chief until an emergency ordinance was passed, waiving the residency requirement. He resigned in less than three months, saying he had a better paying job. His brief tenure was undistinguished. Later he became county assessor and was sentenced to prison in 1931 for theft of $25,000 in county funds.

He is the only one of San Diego's first thirty police chiefs ever to have served time in state prison.

When Moulton resigned on September 3, 1907, Mayor Forward chose a man more qualified. This was a general building contractor, W. T. Neely, who had previous experience in law enforcement in Utah. He had constructed many of the buildings of Madame Katherine Tingley's theosophist complex on Point Loma, and was a member of the city's Board of Public Works.

Neely's appointment as chief was announced the day Moulton quit. Neely was a conscientious, hard-working, competent, and sincere man, well equipped to lead the force.

During Neely's term, in addition to routine problems, the Chinatown area of the Stingaree caused a bit of trouble. Despite sporadic reports of tong wars, which persisted until after World War II, the real thing seems to have happened only once, on Neely's watch. Hit men were imported after Wing Hing was murdered in 1908. Chief Neely, on a tour of Chinatown on an October afternoon, notified merchants that all gambling joints must close, and gave notice to five alleged "highbinders" (Chinese hit men) to get out of town. Neely formulated a policy that crime and disorder must be eliminated in Stingaree Town. But it was to be several years before such a policy could be carried into full effect—and by then Neely was long gone.

A detective division was started. Before 1907, uniformed officers took initial reports, made follow-up investigations, everything. For years they talked of having detectives, but the idea always stalled. That was all changed under Neely. Harry Von Den Berg, a big man with a sloppy moustache, a

In the early winter of 1908 San Diego police mustered thirty-three officers for this picture taken in front of headquarters at 1026 Second Street. Chief William T. Neely is in the center front, with Capt. Bartholomew Moriarty (left) and Sgt. Frank McCarthy (right) all wearing caps. The record clerk, William Gabrielson, in the back row, far left, later became police chief in Honolulu, Hawaii.

deceptively pleasant face, and a flair for big bow ties, became the first detective and later the first detective sergeant.

One of Neely's sons, Harry, a retired Fire Department captain, in an interview in 1978 said his father was active as police chief, but it hurt financially because he made only $125 a month, and it put him out of the building and contracting business.

"The Police Department was fairly honest when father became chief," Harry said. "In the spring of 1909, politicians and preachers took over the town and elected five councilmen for a term of four years. It was a small town, a tough one, and had a small police force. Police did the work they were paid to do, and there was no graft. Old-time cops had a word for graft: 'No money in it,' they used to say.

"My father was not a politician, and when he got enough he resigned as chief and Keno Wilson, an ex-cowboy who did as he was told, took the job."

Police Chief Neely had had enough of politics by May 30,

1909, when he resigned, just before a new city administration took over. He became county building inspector and supervised construction of the County Jail, Balboa Stadium, and the Fine Arts Building in Balboa Park. His exit marked the beginning of a different and far more interesting police department.

The early years of the twentieth century had seen recurrent instability in San Diego's police administration. It was 1909 before the strength and confidence of a police chief, firmly backed by politicians, led the way to permanent expansion.

A new era was about to dawn, an era when horsepower would be created not by oats but by gasoline, and a period in which the rule of law was challenged in this city as it has never been, before or since. It was to be an era in which retired Army Captain John L. Sehon, from a position of power on the City Council, ruled the force with an iron hand—an iron hand that was surely needed.

Chapter 4

JOHN SEHON: ROD OF IRON

The Army's loss was a great gain for the city of San Diego and for the city police. Forced to retire from the Army because of a physical disability, Captain John Leicaster Sehon came to San Diego in 1899, an invalid, to live the remaining days of his life. To this former soldier, who became mayor, councilman, police superintendent, and honored citizen, every San Diego police officer since 1910 owes profound thanks. For Sehon was the father of police benefits.

Sehon was a member of the Common Council when elected mayor in 1905. Two years later in his bid for reelection he lost to John F. Forward. He became a member of the council again, and in 1909 under the newly adopted modified commission plan, was named superintendent of police, health, and morals. Until his death in 1913, "he ruled the underworld of the city with a rod of iron," Judge W. A. Sloane said in a eulogy. "The lawless element knew he was absolutely fair, and both feared and respected him."

Capt. John L. Sehon, father of police benefits.

Before Sehon took charge of police, an officer injured on duty was laid off without pay, and had to pay doctor and hospital bills out of his own pocket. If he were sick, it was the same old story—no work, no pay. There were no death benefits, nor was there a relief fund or an organization to help them in times of distress.

Sehon changed all this, and he was destined to lead a dedicated group of police officers through the most difficult time ever for law enforcement in San Diego, a time of violence when law and order teetered on the verge of collapse and anonymous bands of vigilantes roamed the streets.

His years as leader of police were times not only of violence but also of civic reform. Mayor Grant Conard called for closing unlawful resorts, justice for all, and enforcement of all city laws. Conard warned that no man was above the law. Stern words, these, but words of a politician who knew what the city wanted.

In his history *This Fantastic City*, Shelley Higgins describes Sehon as "a bristling, big fellow, crisply greying. A retired Army officer, he preserved an unyielding military bearing. Even his mustache was martial." A Southerner, he was born in Atlanta, Georgia, and was graduated from a Missouri military academy. He was appointed a U. S. Army second lieutenant. When the United States declared war on Spain in 1898, he was sent to San Francisco, bound for the Philippines as an infantry captain. He was retired when Bright's disease was discovered in a medical examination. A year later he came to San Diego and first entered public service April 7, 1903, when he was elected to the Board of Delegates. As mayor-elect in 1905 he seized the office by climbing up and into a second-story window of City Hall, ending a bitter court fight in which opponents claimed his Army pension barred him from civil office.

The time-honored custom of municipal government by an aldermanic body from wards was abolished in San Diego when citizens adopted a modified Galveston (Texas) commission form of government effective in May 1909. They hoped it would produce an honest, efficient, and more progressive administration. This charter revision provided for distribution

Mrs. Ida Rooker Griffin, left, was appointed matron by Police Chief Wilson on Christmas Eve, 1912, the first woman employed full-time by the department. In 1919, she married Capt. Arthur R. Hill, who became the fifteenth police chief in 1929. Women who followed her in police service are pictured here. Center, Anna Wise, employed as a matron June 17, 1915, and right, Mrs. Olga A. Nelson, one of the first policewomen, appointed April 22, 1926.

of the executive and administrative powers among the five councilmen, with each becoming a superintendent of a city department. Sehon got the plum—police, health, and morals. He also was chosen by fellow councilmen as their first president.

After taking the gavel as council president, Sehon nominated Jefferson Wilson, better known as "Keno" Wilson, to be chief of police. Wilson was a respected veteran of the force and a man who comes down in history as "tall in the saddle." His appointment was promptly approved.

Sehon and Wilson were to make an excellent law enforcement team. The report for their first eight months of work in 1909 indicates they concentrated on better regulation of saloons. A number of licenses were revoked, and some dispensers of liquor were prosecuted for selling to Indians. Drunkenness made up 55 percent of the arrests, but there was an indication of a rapidly accumulating problem, the newfangled automobile, with thirty-eight pinches for violating speed laws. It is in this report that Sehon made several recommendations to improve the welfare and morale of the force:

Retirement of officers on half pay after twenty years of honorable service, or when permanently disabled in line of duty.

Establishment of a police relief fund to provide for sickness and injury benefits.

That a percentage of each reward paid to officers for arrest of wanted persons or recovery of stolen property be retained by the city and put in the relief fund.

That the city authorize funds to purchase a motorized patrol wagon; hire additional detectives; buy new handguns of uniform pattern; adopt the Bertillon identification system; and establish an electric call system for the patrol division.

That two motorcycle officers be added to the force.

This was a new classification; cycle officers could cover the outlying sections faster, and they could also better enforce the speed laws.

The years 1910–1911 would bring police the first headquarters station ever built expressly for the department's use, and in addition a solid building designed and constructed as a city jail.

Sehon inherited an urgent problem when he became police superintendent. Police had moved out of the City Hall at Fifth and G and had leased quarters on Second Street just north of Broadway (D Street). But they still needed more room. Builder J. C. Rice came up with the answer: he would build a new station house on Second Street between F and G streets and lease it to the city. His proposal was accepted.

The lease on the old station expired early in 1910, and the *Union* reported on January 16 that police planned to occupy a "handsome home" about February 15. It was a two-

Police matrons Jennie Bennett, appointed March 1, 1916, Mrs. J. L. Gordon, appointed Dec. 31, 1919, and Mrs. Roberta W. Winter, a clerk in the identification bureau, appointed March 2, 1916.

story plaster and frame building, with large mission-style windows in front. Offices for the chief, captain, detectives, sergeant, and clerk were on the front of the ground floor, with an assembly room for patrolmen, lockers at the rear, and a bathroom with tubs and two showers.

The second floor housed the city justice courtroom and chambers for the justice and police superintendent. Provision was made for space to install a Bertillon identification system and a studio for taking photographs and a darkroom for developing negatives.

On the rear of the lot a garage was built, which would prove valuable if the department ever acquired an automotive patrol wagon. Stalls were provided in the garage for horses and the leased patrol wagon. Above was a loft for storage of property and bicycles.

Wilson's annual report for 1910 shows $125 monthly rent on the building. The police budget for the year was $53,277.88, including $870 to establish a makeshift identification bureau, $35,547 for regular officers' salaries, and $928 for special officers (who were paid $1 a day).

A new city jail was born out of necessity when in the fall of 1910 Sheriff Fred M. Jennings told city officials the County Jail, used also to house police prisoners, was taxed to capacity. To relieve the crowded conditions, the city must make other arrangements. For years the city had used the County Jail for prisoners, first paying a nominal charge of $10 a month, a fee

increased later to $50 and finally to $100.

So a modern jail was built next to the new headquarters on Second Street at a cost of nearly $25,000. The new City Jail was a one-story, poured concrete structure, 96 by 41 feet, with a neoclassic facade. One side provided quarters for women—a room for a matron and three "female" cells—as well as three felony cells and the kitchen. The other side housed the jail office and a booking area, a detention/hospital room, a "sobering up" room, and five cells for misdemeanor male prisoners.

A *Union* reporter described a hygienic feature: "Vagrants, hoboes, common drunks, all will be required to take baths."

Operation of the new jail required a matron. In the past, officers' wives had been used on a part-time basis when needed. Chief Wilson appointed the first full-time woman employee of the force, Mrs. Ida Rooker Griffin, the widow of former County Supervisor John Griffin, who had represented the northern part of the county.

In 1911 the department spent $2,050 for its first automobile, $628 for two motorcycles, and $650 for a patrol wagon and a team of horses.

The stage was set for great improvements in the Police Department, and new capability would be needed in the tumultuous days ahead, when law enforcement in the city was stretched to the breaking point.

Top: A year after this picture was taken in front of the police station at 1026 Second Street, the man mounted on a horse at far right, Jefferson Keno Wilson, a legend among lawmen, was to become San Diego's tenth chief. The other horsemen are, left to right, Jack Golden, Lewis M. Simms, and George H. Pringle. Standing with eight officers, at left, is Sgt. Frank W. McCarthy.
Above: George H. Pringle, who served from 1894 to 1935.
Right: Paul Plaisted, Ida Griffin and Pat Oviatt in front of the the old city jail on Second Street between F and G Streets.

Chapter 5

KENO: TALL IN THE SADDLE

I f Jefferson "Keno" Wilson had any hint of the stormy times ahead for the Police Department, he might have asked himself, "What price glory?" on being offered the job as chief. But those who knew him say he would have tightened his belt, clamped his gaunt jaws together, and "had a go at it."

To use the phrase of a later chief of police, Wesley Sharp, who lived through those days, "All hell broke loose in San Diego," and indeed it did.

Fortunately Wilson, at six feet three inches, was both "tall in the saddle" and tall in his handling of the force in a critical period in the city's history. Some of this was due to rapid growth, some to the sudden emergence of the Auto Age, some to the dawn of technology that would provide lawmen with many scientific tools, and much to the social unrest of the times, which led to the Industrial Workers of the World (IWW) troubles of 1912.

In its obituary on Keno on September 25, 1934, the *Union* said it all:

Jefferson Keno Wilson. Pioneer Western lawman, he wore a badge forty-nine years, from Oceanside constable to San Diego chief, and near the end, deputy U.S. marshal.

> The veteran officer was loved and respected by law-abiding citizens and criminals alike because of his fearlessness, kindness and fairness. He was never injured by the hand of a prisoner and he had the reputation of always "getting his man."
>
> As head of the police force when San Diego underwent the greatest period of turbulence, Wilson made an unusually fine record. He governed the Police Department when the old Stingaree district was in power, and he was chief when the Stingaree was abolished.

It was largely due to his active measures as chief of police that IWW trouble in 1912 was brought to decision.

If he thought an officer was right, Keno was fiercely loyal, a mark of all good police chiefs. He was usually quiet and little inclined to talk about other officials or himself, but could become "red hot," as newspapermen liked to phrase it. When District Attorney Harold Utley started an inquiry on a complaint that a youth had been handled roughly by an officer, Keno replied in the press: "He (Utley) can bulldoze others but he can't bulldoze me." But Wilson and Utley united when the IWW troubles began.

Because Keno was reserved and humble, he is the least known of the colorful early-day officers, and San Diego had its share. The late A. E. Jansen, who served the longest of any San Diego police chief before being appointed sheriff, writing in the *San Diego Historical Society Quarterly* in October 1962 about Wilson ("A Lawman's Lawman"), explained why Keno was not well known:

> More would be known of him if it were not for the fact that his modesty amounted almost to bashfulness and it was hard to get him to talk about his past exploits.
>
> It would be amiss if Western movies and pulp magazine thrillers were what robbed us of getting the true Keno Wilson story. But in his later years, when relatives urged him to jot down his memoirs, so thorough was his disgust with the horse opera school of literature that he declined, and when he headed for the last roundup, much of San Diego County's history went with him.

Police Chief Wilson, who was comfortable in the saddle but had to have a chauffeur for his auto because he did not drive, joined his nine-man mounted squad outside the Second Street station between F and G streets sometime late in 1914 as officers prepared for the 1915 Panama-California Exposition.

In addition to his personal courage, he also had the cunning of an Indian scout, one writer contended. His unusual name, Keno, suggests the wild and hectic days of the Old West. He was baptized Jefferson Keener, but he was called Keno from birth.

Keno was born in Visalia, California, and at age eight went to live with an uncle, John Wilson, on a ranch in Denton County, Texas, and remained there until he was seventeen, driving cattle and doing other ranch work. One Sunday while Keno was idling in the ranch yard, Buffalo Bill (William F. Cody) rode in from the north. Keno years later in a newspaper interview recalled this meeting and commented: "He was a fearless man. He came riding down through a lot of wild country, all alone, to buy up ponies and take them north. He could shoot, too. He did a lot of buffalo hunting around the country, and he was a man that everybody liked."

When Keno returned to his native state, he began his long service as a Southern California peace officer, first working as an investigator for two ranches from 1884 to 1886 and then being appointed to his first public job as a deputy constable at Oceanside in 1886.

The *Union*, commenting on Wilson's appointment as chief on May 3, 1909, said, "Wilson always has been considered a hard-working, conscientious officer, fearless, kindly and of sound judgment. His promotion is pleasing to his fellow officers and is popular with businessmen. It is claimed for Wilson that he is better acquainted in the country than any other officer and will give the horse thieves a bad time."

Wes Sharp, who retired as chief in 1968, painted a picture from memory of Wilson:

He was a quiet, grim and reserved man who knew when to keep his mouth shut and who made a good police chief. He was a hero to us kids, a man to behold in the saddle, tall, a ramrod.

All the pioneer Western lawmen had to be men of steel,

and when they used their gun, it was either they killed the outlaw or they got killed. Keno had a reputation as a man who could fire with accuracy and speed. He had to, or die in the early days when he was a constable, marshal, deputy sheriff, and customs collector. Whether it was demonstration of fine shooting or a bit of luck I'll never know, but this is my story of how Keno could shoot. My Dad ran a livery stable at Ninth and Island and knew Keno real well. One day I stood beside my Dad outside the stable while he talked to Keno. Suddenly a man came out of a house across the street and Wilson shouted, "Stop, I want to talk to you," and the man started running. Keno whipped out his pistol and fired one shot at the running man.

The man just went up in the air and came down flat on the sidewalk. We all ran over to him, and you won't believe me—Keno had shot the heel off one shoe of the man and didn't hurt him a bit. He got his prisoner.

Another story old-timers loved to tell about Wilson involved Maggie Dangerfield, a lower Fifth Street character. She was under arrest one day by Wilson and other officers, when she bit Keno's hand and he rapped her across the head with his billy club. She reared back and yelled at him, "Gentlemen don't strike a lady!" There was no grand jury investigation, and Maggie went to the hoosegow.

The San Diego Historical Society possesses all the badges worn by Keno Wilson during his 49-year career as a San Diego county and city peace officer. They include the sergeant's badge he wore at the end of his police career; his San Diego chief's star; the city marshal's shield he wore at Oceanside, where he succeeded his brother; another as deputy marshal of San Diego. Of the eight badges displayed, Keno's favorite was a U. S. Customs badge made from a Mexican silver peso, acquired while he was serving as a deputy collector-inspector at Campo.

Left: The first motorcycle officers began police patrol in San Diego in 1909. In this 1914 photo the rider at far left is James Patrick, the acting police chief in 1917 and chief in 1919. Right: Motorcycle Officer Leonard Freshour is shown on his belt-driven Excelsor motor with Presto Lite lamp, ca. 1915.

On the night of July 3, 1889, Keno, as an Oceanside city constable, was on foot patrol with his brother, City Marshal Charlie C. Wilson. Around 1 a.m. the Wilson brothers heard shots and breaking of glass near the old St. Cloud Hotel, where a small crowd of brawlers afoot and mounted, had gathered. As they approached they saw a man on horseback. He was John Murray, a Texan who a year before had threatened some day to get the drop on the marshal. Murray was holding a kerosene lamp taken from one of the street lights. Charlie asked the crowd of brawlers for orderly behavior.

The marshal grabbed Murray's horse by the bridle and Murray, who held the lamp in one hand and a pistol in the other, threw the lamp at Charlie's head and shot him through the heart. The marshal was dead when he slumped to the ground.

Keno fired three shots at the fleeing Murray but missed the suspect, who fled east in the dark.

News of the cold-blooded slaying brought lawmen on the run from all over Southern California to join in the manhunt for the slayer. The marshal of Santa Ana created a stir when he put his horse on the express car of the southbound passenger train, climbed in, and highballed to Oceanside. The San Diego County Board of Supervisors authorized a reward of $500 for Murray's capture. A number of search parties were being organized when word was received that Murray, exhausted and starving, had appeared at the ranch of James H. Griffin, nine miles east of Oceanside, and after surrendering his pistol, said he had shot the marshal.

Thomas Weller, the San Diego city poundmaster, who was in Oceanside, quickly organized a party and they went

riding hell-bent east. Before leaving, Weller telegraphed Police Chief Coyne in San Diego: "Murray caught. Send men at once to meet team on the Poway road. Parties leaving to catch and lynch him."

Knowing that a lynch mob had formed in Oceanside, heavily armed men spirited Murray into San Diego in a spring wagon. After an uneventful trip, they delivered the prisoner at the County Jail.

Murray was found guilty of first-degree murder and sentenced to death. An appeal was filed with the state Supreme Court. The case dragged on. The court said local newspapers had unduly inflamed public opinion against Murray. The verdict was set aside. A new trial resulted in a second conviction and death by hanging was ordered for April 14, 1892. Murray died in the County Jail of natural causes a few weeks before the execution date. But that didn't end it for Keno. He didn't talk about it, but his friends said his brother's death haunted Wilson all his years.

So great was Keno's reputation with fellow lawmen, he was long remembered and termed the greatest professional of them all. He was shy but dignified, masculine but gentle. When Sehon tapped him to lead the force, Keno had nearly nine years on the department, mostly on horse patrol. He was forty-six, lean, rawboned, with a drooping mustache, a taciturn man.

Keno made good newspaper copy, so some stories of how he acquired prized possessions exist in files. One was a beautiful pearl-handle Colt .45 revolver that had been bequeathed to him by the chief of the Pala Indian tribe. After the old chief died, his sons brought the pistol to San Diego and

Supervising officers in 1912 when this picture was taken wore caps with ranks clearly shown on the front. Patrolmen still had pith hats carried over from early times. This group, in front of headquarters in the 700 block of Second Street, were, left to right, George Lendemood, Rollie Heddens, unidentified, Sgt. Harvey Shepherd, D.D. Mullinis, Henry Stevens, and James Best.

ceremoniously presented it to Keno.

Another prize was acquired when Buffalo Bill Cody came to town with his famous Wild West show. Wilson reminded Cody how they first met in Texas when Keno was a boy. Cody remembered, and not long before the famous showman died, he presented Wilson with a watch fob bearing the likeness of his famous self and his almost equally famous protégé, Pawnee Bill.

During research for this history, the author found an envelope in material given the Historical Society by Wilson's survivors. Inside was a typewritten sheet of paper, probably the only résumé Keno took time to write. This record of his colorful career is terse, to the point, no-nonsense, and without color. Here it is:

> 1884 to 1886—Special Investigator, Detective work for Los Bolsas and Stearns Ranchos Companys. I was riding over the two Ranches of over two hundred thousand acres of land that over two hundred persons had been living on as squatters.

> June 6th, 1886—Sworn in as Deputy Constable under Will Griffin, Constable at Oceanside, California.

> Nov. 6th, 1888—I was elected Constable at General Election at Oceanside for term two years.

> Nov. 26th, 1890—Elected Constable at Oceanside, two-year term.

> July 16, 1889—I was appointed City Marshal at Oceanside by the City Trustees. April 14, 1890, I was elected City Marshal at Oceanside, term two years.

> January 1st, 1893—I was appointed Deputy Sheriff under Sheriff Ben P. Hill at San Diego for term two years. In 1894 I held the office of Deputy U. S. Marshal for San Diego Co., under N. A. Coverrubia, U. S. Marshal, held the same until Jan. 28, 1894.

> Jan 22nd, 1894—I was appointed Deputy Collector & Inspt. U. S. Customs under John C. Fisher, Customs Collector at San Diego. I was stationed at Campo, Calif., and patrolled the line from Dulzura to Yuma, Arizona. I was Deputy. Col. & Inspt., U. S. Customs to 1898, until change of administration, and Collectors of U. S. Customs.

> My Record in San Diego Police Department.

> Dec. 18, 1899, appointed patrolman. From May 1900 to May 3, 1909, was mounted patrolman. May 1, 1909, appointed Chief of Police by the City Councilmen. I was Chief of Police for four terms two years each. Balance of the time was desk sergeant. I was in the San Diego Police Department 25 years,

The year is 1912 and life in San Diego is far from hectic. The City Jail had been opened a short time before and the police station, on the right, was occupied in 1910. The horse and buggy in front of the jail were being eliminated by the noisy and dangerous automobile, which a detective is examining on the right.

six months and five days.

May 25, 1926, I was appointed Deputy U. S. Marshal for San Diego County under United States Marshal Albert C. Sittel. July 1, 1929, appointed a second time. Third appointment, sworn in Sept. l, 1932, under Marshal Sittel.

Some historian said Wilson was a good policeman but a poor politician, but his résumé listing his four terms as chief is convincing proof he was good at being both. He served more than seven years as top man, some of them the roughest years in police history.

Early in his administration Wilson proved he could adjust the budget, an ability he had in common with all chiefs. Shortly after he took command there was a deficit in funds, and he asked all officers to contribute $1 each from their salaries for gunpowder so weekly target practices could continue.

By year's end Keno was busy ridding the city of "Weary Willies," as tramps were called. Wilson, like all chiefs since the railroad came to the city, had inherited the problem of hoboes flocking to San Diego on freight trains. Earlier, when convicted of vagrancy and often petty theft, they were used on the city chain gang. An old story about the use of the chain gang in Stingaree Town is often recounted by historians. The story tells of an enterprising policeman who figured a way to pad his salary. He took the chain gang to the Stingaree district and told the madams he had orders to clean up back yards. He charged a fee of two bucks per girl working in a house, which he collected after the yard was clean, pocketing the money. He got away with this shady business for some time.

Two hundred tramps were picked up for vagrancy in a two-week period in December 1895. The hoboes had a permanent camp then in the Sweetwater Valley, with a big tent for meetings, brush-covered huts, a regular cook, and foraging parties for food. There was another smaller camp near Twelfth Street in San Diego. The invasions of hoboes in the late 1880s got so bad the city had to hire five extra officers at $75 each per month during the winters to combat the problem.

Between 1905 and 1907, a speed limit for automobiles and motorcycles was set at three miles and later at six miles an hour between Cedar and E streets and Third and Seventh streets. At that time runaway horses were the most dangerous of traffic hazards, and fast cars spooked the animals. A motorcycle officer was hired in 1909. Then five patrolmen were assigned to direct traffic at the busiest downtown intersections, as it became fashionable for the rich to own cars.

Progress engulfed the force by 1910. One custom of the day enabled prisoners to ride in style to jail. Those unable to walk were transported to the pokey in a hack, drawn by a pair of coach horses, with the cab driver wearing gloves and a derby hat. Taxpayers footed the bill.

This stylish mode of handling prisoners was changed by 1910: Wilson's report for that year shows a rental of a patrol wagon and team for $100 the first month and $150 each for the remaining months of the year. Jerry MacMullen, historian and former executive director of the Historical Society, once described this "Black Maria" as a grim, black-curtained affair, with square kerosene lamps and a rotary gong to clear the way.

It went clanging around town from the old station on Second just north of Broadway. Passengers were varied. One trip, the paddy wagon might bring in merely the unconscious form of John Doe Drunk No.1—if he were the first arrested that day—[or] it could be a full load of unhappy citizens who had been gathered up on a raid on a fan-tan game, down Chinatown-way.

If things got out of hand in some waterfront saloon, a telephone call brought the "law" on the run, with an imposing clatter of hoofs and bells, to take on a load of foremast hands from some lumber schooner or deep-water sailing ship in from a six-month voyage.

MacMullen's description conjures up a picture of the Keystone Cops.

Chief Wilson wiped out the yearly rental of $1,650 for team and paddy wagon in 1911 when the city bought a wagon and team for $650. The era of the horse was dying. The same year the city also purchased an auto for the police chief for $2,050, a Dodge touring car. (The chief had to get authorization for a chauffeur, as he could not drive.) By 1914 autos were used on patrol, an ominous note. It was to presage what was to come in 1916—stabling of all horses. Progress again was plowing under one of the most inspiring sights, a cop on a horse.

The late Jack Golden, who joined the force on January

San Diego's police detectives in 1911 were not specialized, but took any case on the roster, from petty theft to homicide. There are some famous old-timers of the force in this picture. Capt. Bartholomew Moriarty, who was in charge of all operations, is seated. Standing, left to right, Frank F. Boucherie, Harvey F. Shepherd (later first lieutenant of the force), Helim O. Fish, Frank C. Wisler, Joseph E. Myers (who would become chief of detectives in 1912), Will C. Carse, Bert Thorpe, and Pierre Boisseree.

12, 1908, recalled how miserable horse patrol could be in foul weather. One rainy day in the 1950s, during his long retirement, he took a walk and came upon a parked police car. Inside, the patrol officer was working on his daily report, warm and dry, while the windshield wipers kept the windshield clear. Jack rapped on the window, the patrolman lowered it, and Golden introduced himself as a retired old-timer and said, "I just want to tell you how lucky you modern officers are. In my day all we had on horse patrol was a poncho to protect us against rain, and some mounted men got comfort and warmth from a bottle. Often I patrolled all of Logan Heights, alone, no radio to call for help, just me—the law—against whatever turned up."

Every man on the force was turned out early on the morning of July 1, 1910, in a search for a discharged, deranged city fireman, who had shot and killed two firemen and wounded others responding to a false alarm at Second and Spruce.

Chief Wilson led officers to a hotel where the gunman's wife and two-year-old son were found dead, their heads crushed. The slayer committed suicide a few hours later in Horton Plaza when recognized by a policeman. The *Union's* next-day story called it "one of the most awful crimes in the history of San Diego County."

There were continued rumbles that the reform government was about to clean up the Stingaree district. On March 4, 1910, the press headlined, "A Clean Sweep Promised." But the move was stalled. More troublesome matters were to occupy the time of police.

Chapter 6
DARKEST HOUR: IWW TROUBLES

The year 1912 was the most turbulent and memorable in the history of the San Diego Police Department. First there was the Industrial Workers of the World (IWW) uprising, a free speech fight that drew national attention. Later the same year, San Diego's famous Stingaree red-light district was shut down permanently.

At the time, most San Diegans believed themselves fortunate to have that man of iron and leader of the reform element, John Sehon, as police superintendent, and that seasoned veteran, Police Chief Keno Wilson, as the "long arm of the law."

In 1906 when the IWW (whose members were commonly called "Wobblies") first appeared in San Diego, business leaders paid little attention to this radical labor union with only a few local members. It was a rival to the American Federation of Labor. The IWW, an industrial union, attacked the craft unions of the AFL as viciously as it attacked the capitalistic system. The AFL viewed the IWW members as anarchists.

In 1900 and continuing for a decade, a building boom gave a big boost to San Diego labor unions, which began to flex their muscles, causing businessmen to consider plans to curtail unionists who might become troublesome later and could have an impact on business during the 1915 Panama-California Exposition in Balboa Park. This event, years in the planning, was to be the capstone of a real estate boom that San Diegans believed would make their city one of the great ones on the Pacific Coast of North America. The city and its leaders extended themselves in this great project and were utterly determined that it must succeed.

The San Diego IWW members joined insurgents in Tijuana in the Mexican Revolution of 1910, disbanding their local union, but after Mexican federal troops made Baja California secure for the Republic, the Wobblies re-established Local 13 in San Diego and appealed to any workingman regardless of occupation to join.

In 1910 and continuing into 1911, Local 13 organized workers and was blamed for strikes. The IWW sought to organize city employees and transit workers. Businessmen and civic leaders began to consider the need for an ordinance to control street speaking in order to combat the Wobblies, who were using street-corner soapboxes to advance their movement.

For twenty years the area around Fifth and E streets had been dedicated to open-air meetings, with vehicular traffic prohibited at night. Radio and television were far in the future, and these informal gatherings were popular in the evening, drawing crowds seeking entertainment. Folks gossiped among themselves, traded news, and listened to speakers voicing opinions on many subjects both popular and unpopular. A typical evening would find the Salvation Army's little band playing to attract a crowd, a Socialistic orator as the next "attraction," then an astrologer predicting the future, and a Single-Taxer hammering away. By late 1911, the Wobblies regularly were singing their songs before a speaker who stood on a makeshift platform on "Soapbox Row."

By October 1911, leaders of the city and businessmen had their fill of the IWW. Eighty-five of these leaders invited Harrison Gray Otis, owner of the *Los Angeles Times* and a leader in the statewide organization, the Merchants and Manufacturers Association, to speak at a dinner meeting at the Grant Hotel. Otis hated all union men and called them traitors to their country. His huge land holdings in Mexico were threatened by the Mexican Revolution, which the IWW had aided and abetted. He urged San Diego to take up the cause against all labor unions, and particularly against the IWW.

Specifically, he suggested the city pass a law forbidding street meetings. Otis also appeared before the county grand jury, and that group asked the City Council to pass an anti–street speaking ordinance. At first the council was cool to the idea, but after a meeting with supporters on December 8, council members said they would consider the proposal. Then, five days later, a counter-petition was presented to the council and some thought the idea was dead. It wasn't.

Soapbox Row was closed to vehicles in the evening, but on the evening of Saturday, January 6, 1912, an auto was driven through, some said with the horn sounding continuously to drown out an IWW speaker. This car, driven by Robert Walsh, a real estate man and deputy constable, was rocked. Someone slashed one of the tires with a pocket knife. The IWW speaker told the crowd to leave the car alone, as it appeared to be an effort to provoke an incident.

An incident it became. Walsh drove away, but soon returned, escorted by Chief Wilson, Superintendent of Police/Councilman Sehon, and Detective Joseph Myers, a sergeant who three days later would be promoted to captain of detectives. Before the police arrived, the IWW speaker had concluded his speech and left the scene, together with most of

Left: This photograph captures a famous moment in the civil disorder of that year, the use of fire hose by firemen and police to disperse a crowd formed near the city jail, known as "the water cure." Note the indifference to the violent action by the woman on the sidewalk at right. Below: During the 1912 IWW troubles in San Diego, this scene was a common sight: a roundup of incoming protesters. Removed from freight trains, they were formed in columns and under guard marched to a city lockup. Later when all facilities were overflowing, prisoners were even marched to a stockade which was built in Sorrento Valley, sixteen miles north. The mounted officer (identified by star) in the lead at left is in charge of this detail, assisted by the other mounted flankers and rear guard, who were civilians sworn in as "specials" at $1 a day.

the Wobblies. A Single-Taxer had mounted his makeshift podium across the street. The officers jerked the speaker off the soapbox and, with Sehon looking on, used force to clear the area. One IWW member was recognized and arrested.

This was enough for the City Council, and the anti–street speaking ordinance passed on Monday, January 8, with an emergency clause which gave the measure immediate effect, as normally it would not become law for thirty days. This

law prohibited any kind of public meeting in a designated area in the center of the downtown area. IWW and other speakers were permitted to hold meetings elsewhere, but the Wobblies raised the cry of suppression of speech.

Sehon acted promptly, ordering Chief Wilson to enforce the ordinance "down to the last letter," and Keno obeyed this order, down to the last letter.

The expected confrontation between police and the IWW speakers was averted on the night of January 10 when City Attorney Charles M. Andrews told Sehon and Wilson he believed the emergency clause of the new law might successfully be challenged in court. The city leaders decided to wait for thirty days. The Union said police were powerless to act. The liberals of the city, who had voted for Sehon as a

municipal reform candidate, began to wonder. The thirty-day waiting period ran out February 8. That night in preparation for a parade by those opposed to the "Soapbox gag rule," every available policeman was on duty, sixty regulars and some specials hired at $1 a shift.

They were stationed along a parade line of march which Superintendent Sehon laid out for the protesters. A group of police officers led the way. But at the designated end of the parade at Seventh and B streets, the marchers defied police orders and continued walking until they faced officers on lines at Sixth and E, blocking entrance into Soapbox Row. Some marchers reached Fifth Street and, as they started to mount a platform, officers placed them under arrest.

Laura Payne Emerson, wife of a jeweler, was a popular

Constables in 1912. They were stationed south of San Clemente by the county Board of Supervisors at a blockage point to turn back undesirable persons during the troubled period.

speaker for the IWW, and when the trouble thickened, she was in the middle of it. Forty-one persons were arrested, including Mrs. Emerson and two other women.

The battle had been joined between "free speechers" and the city. Next morning, instead of being charged with a misdemeanor violation of the street-speaking ordinance, defendants faced charges of conspiracy to disobey the law, a felony. Bail was fixed at $750 cash or $1,500 bond. Since leadership would be needed in the struggle with authorities, bails were posted and Laura Emerson and other leaders were released. The rank and file were remanded to the County Jail.

The press reported that, of the forty-one arrested the first night, twelve were penniless, seventeen had no more than $1, and only two had more than $10. Of these forty-one, only seven were eventually convicted as charged. Fifteen more arrests were made the next night, and by the end of the week the total passed one hundred. The Wobblies were carrying the fight, and on February 13 Sehon issued this order: "Round up all male vagrants and hoboes."

Chief Wilson's report for 1912 shows 525 arrests related to the IWW troubles from February through May. From a high of 137 detentions in March, they dropped to twenty in May. Except for the handful of leaders needed to direct the fight, all the "criminal conspiracy" prisoners refused bail and demanded jury trials. By the end of March the new City Jail, built to hold sixty prisoners, bulged with more than 150. Many of these

men were veterans of free speech battles in other cities. They had expected to be arrested on arrival in San Diego, and they were.

Rumors spread that Wobblies in the thousands were headed for San Diego. Spurred on by International IWW headquarters, the local Wobbly leaders predicted "between 5,000 and 10,000" would swell their ranks.

The main route into this isolated city was the railroad from the north. The first of many city details of mounted officers, regulars and specials, were assigned to the Sorrento Valley, along the tracks thirteen miles north of the downtown area, to check everyone using rails or roads, and turn back anyone suspected of being a vagrant or sympathetic to the IWW cause.

By the end of February both the city and the county jails in San Diego were crowded beyond capacity, and the overflow of those arrested was being sent to jails in Orange County and San Bernardino County. It became plain that the IWW plan was to bankrupt the city by keeping arrested members in jails, clogging court calendars, and in general disrupting the due process of law.

The *Union* predicted San Diego would be victorious over the Wobblies, even if every county jail in the state had to be used to detain them. Because San Diego was the southwest corner of the nation, and the only access by rail was from the north, it was not difficult to "cut them off at the pass."

This copy of an old lantern slide shows an IWW orator identified as "Wobblie Jack White" entertaining a crowd on E Street downtown during the early days of the disorders. To residents this practice was known as "soapboxing." In this crowd are police detectives in civilian clothing keeping an eye on the proceedings.

County supervisors established mounted constables at San Onofre, just inside the San Diego County line, as guards on both the roads and the rail line. Going into March, city authorities thought the tide of Wobblies had been stemmed.

The City Jail had drawn curious spectators from the beginning of the trouble. IWW leaders took advantage of the crowds to mount temporary platforms and denounce "the brutality of the Cossacks," their favorite name for police. An officer snorted when these charges were aired: " We work sixteen hours a day, get little sleep, and it is most difficult to keep one's temper when bums spit in your face." Once Chief Wilson called Wobblies "worse than animals," and for Keno that was mighty strong language.

The *Tribune* also dehumanized the Wobblies in an editorial: "Hanging is none too good for them. They would be much better off dead, for they are absolutely useless in the human economy, they are the waste material of creation and should be drained off into the sewer of oblivion, there to rot in cold obstruction like any other excrement."

On what would have been a peaceful Sunday afternoon except for the IWW troubles, a crowd estimated at up to 5,000 gathered on March 10 outside City Jail. Lulu Wightman and Laura Emerson were "soapboxing" the good crowd. The location was outside the zone in which street meetings were pro-

hibited, but Chief Wilson did not like the "feel" outside the jail. He was an old lawman who paid a lot of attention to hunches, one of the best tools of his trade. He turned in a fire alarm, and firemen responded in strength.

Wilson then ordered 1.5-inch fire hoses turned on the crowd when they refused to disperse. At first firemen aimed the high-pressure water from the hoses at the feet of the crowd as they advanced. In the end they let one and all have the full force of the water, in what was to become known in police and fire history as the "water cure."

Thousands of postcards were subsequently sold showing the Wobblies being given the treatment. San Diegans were generally proud of their policemen and firemen. One picture illustrates the scornful attitude of many citizens: It shows a well-dressed woman, her long skirt nearly dragging the ground, walking calmly along the sidewalk as water from fire hoses sweeps the street only a few feet from her. She is contemptuous, looking straight ahead, ignoring the action.

For three hours this unbelievable struggle continued. False alarms poured into the fire alarm system. By nightfall a police officer was stationed beside every fire alarm box downtown. By coming of night, the stubborn remnant of the crowd, dripping wet and bruised, left the field of battle to rally at Germanic Hall. This was the only use of fire hoses to disperse crowds during the IWW turmoil. The tactic was not repeated.

San Diego city and county jails and lockups in two surrounding counties were full. The council on March 12 authorized building a stockade in Sorrento Valley for temporary detention. Sehon and Wilson decided on selective arrests, and the jail crowding eased.

Using the "move on" ordinance passed in February, police broke up street crowds anywhere in the city. The nightstick was in evidence in police actions. Captain of Detectives Joe Myers summed up the mood: "We tried to treat them [Wobblies] with forbearance; now they can move on or look out."

Mean tempers resulted from working shifts of fourteen to sixteen hours, infrequent catnaps in the station house in place of regular sleep, going without normal food, and facing an almost impossible task. The attrition rate for a department of sixty men (when trouble started) was the highest, in terms of percentage, in history: Wilson recorded fourteen resignations of officers. When they could take it no longer, they turned in their badges. But another man was there to take over. Wilson's 1912 report said: "There have been forty-eight appointments made, including one surgeon, one matron, and two specials."

There were rumors that forty thousand Wobblies were ready to descend on the beleaguered city. County supervisors swore in forty-five mounted constables and on April 4 they were deployed at the San Onofre blockade point, reinforced by vigilantes.

The next day one hundred vagrants were pulled off a freight train by constables and turned over to vigilantes, who made the detained men kneel and kiss the flag, sing the national anthem, and then run a gantlet of "enforcers" swinging paddles. They were then allowed to run back into Orange County, with a warning not to return. These were known to citizens as ceremonious beatings, to Wobblies as just plain brutality.

False alarms sounded often. The *New York Call* on March 16, 1914, summing up the IWW troubles, said authorities became excited one night over a report of an IWW camp in Balboa Park. A roundup was prepared, but it was discovered this camp was only the campfire of a Boy Scout outing. Carroll W. West, late retired superintendent of the police garage, in a 1977 interview, said he was in the Boy Scout troop which had an outing behind the city shops on the old dike and during the rioting they had a big bonfire and someone called police to report Wobblies camping. "They sent the patrol wagon with two mounted policemen and surrounded us, until they sheepishly discovered we were only small boys," West recalled.

Kidnappings were blamed on vigilantes. The most publicized was the Emma Goldman incident. This well-known anarchist speaker had conducted funeral services in Los Angeles for an elderly Wobbly who died in a hospital after becoming ill in the San Diego City Jail. She said authorities refused to permit services to be held in San Diego.

Ignoring Chief Wilson's message strongly urging them to stay away from San Diego, Goldman and her manager, Ben Reitman, came to the city by train on May 14 and were met by a crowd at the depot. They went by auto to the Grant Hotel. While she was being ordered by Wilson to leave town, her business manager was kidnapped by vigilantes and taken into the north county. At a remote spot, he was tarred and a lighted cigar was used to burn "IWW" on his buttocks. He was released, wearing only underwear and his vest. He walked to Escondido and took a train back to Los Angeles, where Emma Goldman was anxiously awaiting word. He later said the vigilantes told him the only reason they didn't kill him was that they had given Keno Wilson their promise not to.

Abraham R. Sauer, sixty-five, editor of the weekly *San Diego Herald*, also was kidnapped after his paper supported the free speech movement and he attacked police in print for brutality. Vigilantes took him prisoner April 5 in front of his home, hustled him into a car, and drove twenty miles into the back country. He said they tied a rope around his neck, threw one end over a tree branch, and lifted him from the ground, but then lowered him to the ground again. He was frightened but uninjured, and promised not to return to San Diego nor reveal the identities of the vigilantes. He did return, but he kept his promise not to name names.

It wasn't only the police who winked at and shielded the vigilantes. District Attorney Harold Utley made no statement and took no action except to deputize several hundred citizens to take the Wobbly prisoners out of town. Only Sheriff Fred M. Jennings showed any inclination to take on the vigilantes, sending out officers to search for the kidnapped Sauer when city police were slow to act.

Don Stewart in *Frontier Port* wrote of the vigilante days and nights: "If the vigilantes ever had one formal leader, I don't know who he was, but I do know there were a lot of substantial citizens in it."

The names of many prominent men were mentioned as vigilante members in radical newspapers published outside the city. Strong suspicion focused on John D. Spreckels, who owned the *Union*, the *Tribune*, the transit system, and a good deal of the town. Certain law enforcement officers were also believed to have joined the vigilante ranks and a *Union* reporter was named as a vigilante captain. None of this was ever officially confirmed and the names did not appear in local newspapers.

The mood of the city did not need any further aggravation, but it came anyway, with a vengeance. The serious wounding of two regular policemen, H. G. Stevens and R. H. Heddon—outside IWW headquarters at Thirteenth and K streets on the night of May 7—aroused the city.

The police account of what happened went as follows:. The IWW headquarters was kept under constant police surveillance; the two officers had this duty when two men jumped out from behind a signboard across the street and opened fire. Stevens was shot twice. As the policemen returned the gunfire, a man, later identified as Joseph Mikolasek, ran from the headquarters and hit Heddon over one eye with an axe. Heddon, his vision obscured by his own blood, went down but managed to shoot his assailant several times.

The wounded Mikolasek walked and crawled two blocks, where he asked the aid of a housewife, who called police. On his deathbed, he said he thought the officers had followed him from a street meeting, where he had been beaten severely. He said he was standing in the doorway when an officer flashed a light in his eyes and ordered him outside. He said the officer opened fire before he could comply, hitting him in the legs. He said he then grabbed the axe, which was lying just inside the doorway, and hit the officer. The Wobblies contended there were no mysterious men behind the billboard and Stevens was shot by mistake by Heddon after Heddon had been dazed by the axe blow.

As Robert Diehl (a candidate for a master's degree at the University of San Diego) said in his 1976 thesis "To Speak or Not to Speak," whatever the facts were, the Wobblies paid dearly for the incident.

When word was received that two wounded officers were

The two San Diego policemen seriously wounded during the IWW troubles of 1912 are pictured here. Rollie M. Hedden, left, was struck on the head with an axe, and Henry G. Stevens, right, was shot twice.

down and needed help, reinforcements flooded the scene. IWW headquarters was surrounded, and five men who were found hiding in the attic were arrested. Two rifles and ammunition were seized. A series of prearranged blasts on the whistle at the lower D Street (Broadway) powerhouse sounded a citywide emergency. All available policemen and vigilantes were mustered. Curious citizens gathered in front of the Second Street police station. Nightsticks were issued to vigilantes. They broke up into groups for patrols, and witnesses said many carried guns. They swept the city. Loiterers were arrested and placed in the Mason Street school and in the Grape Street stockade, recently built. The next day they were transferred to the stockade at Sorrento.

Stewart describes in *Frontier Port* the reaction of Governor Hiram Johnson (who ran for vice president that year on the Progressive Party ticket with Theodore Roosevelt) after vigilantes boldly took over part of law enforcement: "The governor sent Harris Weinstock, of the old Sacramento mercantile firm of Weinstock & Lubin, here to investigate the vigilante committee. He also sent the state attorney general, U. S. Webb. They were both smart men, and I guess it didn't take them long to find that public opinion was almost solidly behind the [vigilante] committee. Nothing came of it. The whole thing was an open defiance of civil authority."

In his published report, Weinstock denounced the IWW first and foremost, "because of its unholy and reckless methods of civil disobedience." But his main recommendation to the governor was that the state attorney general investigate the complaints of the victims of the vigilantes. Weinstock said District Attorney Harold S. Utley displayed "his pronounced hostilities to them and to their causes of complaint." Weinstock condemned any toleration by law enforcement officials of extra-legal vigilante action. No law enforcement action was ever taken against the vigilantes, however.

The district attorney was singularly uncooperative, Weinstock reported, but Police Commissioner Sehon, Chief of Police Wilson and Captain of Detectives Myers "responded most properly and cheerfully" to Weinstock's request for information. He found there was some evidence of needless police

brutality but he said, "Such police officials as I met in San Diego impressed me as being above average in intelligence, in character and in personality."

Diehl summarizes the general feeling toward the police: "In each case the police felt justified in their treatment of the Wobblies. If the normal legal measures were ineffective to deal with the situation, their brute force was required. Urged on by their superior officers, commended for their actions by the leading businessmen and applauded for their behavior by the Spreckels press, the policemen of San Diego could only believe that their methods of dealing with the free speech advocates were right."

Rumors of smallpox halted booking of new prisoners in the City Jail on June 7, 1912. The remaining fifteen IWW inmates pleaded guilty, and each was given a $100 fine and thirty days in jail, suspended. The jails in San Diego, Orange, and San Bernardino Counties were emptied of IWW prisoners. Only those charged with conspiracy and not out on bond remained in the local jail. Activities of police and vigilantes wound down.

The struggle had been costly to the city, but it was of benefit to the Police Department. Citizens were grateful for the dedication of their officers, and did not forget for nearly two decades: it was not until Prohibition days that the respect earned in 1912 was eroded.

In 1910 Wilson had a department of thirty officers. A year later he added eleven more and in 1912 ended up with thirty-four more personnel, even though fourteen resigned during the disorders. By 1913 the Police Department could field eighty-seven officers.

The force had nearly tripled in three years. But there was a cost. The rule of law suffered when officers and law enforcement officials abdicated their sworn duty to the law and the Constitution. Vigilante justice was a throwback to cowboy justice, out of place in a modern city. Serious scars had been inflicted upon the Police Department's relationship to a segment of the citizenry. And lasting damage had been done to the national image of San Diego as a serene little city by a sunlit sea.

Chapter 7
THE OFFICERS ORGANIZE

Although the drive to suppress the IWW was anti-labor, it led indirectly to the organization of a special type of independent labor union for police officers. One of the positive results of the IWW troubles was the realization by citizens of the lack of adequate benefits for sick and injured officers of the police force. This spurred civic support and brought about the creation of a benevolent society.

Police Superintendent Sehon's 1909 request for benefits bore fruit the next year. City councilmen approved the diversion of a third of any reward monies paid to officers to a police relief fund, as Sehon had recommended. But this provided very little relief, according to George W. Churchman, retired police lieutenant: "I joined in the middle of January 1912, shortly after the IWW troubles began," Churchman said in a 1981 interview. "When I became sick with typhoid fever and pneumonia, the relief fund paid me $13 a month, not enough even in those days to live on. When you became sick, the pay check stopped at the end of the month. Many of us went back to duty still half sick, so we would have some money to live on."

Two days after the May 7 wounding of Officers Stevens and Heddon in front of the IWW headquarters, John D. Spreckels offered "to subscribe from $200 to $500 toward establishment of a police relief fund to care for members of the force injured on duty."

In a subsequent story on May 13, 1912, the press told citizens the salary of a policeman hurt on duty stopped at the end of the month, and officers had to pay their own hospital and doctor bills. "The police, who have done such effective work during the uprising of the Industrial Workers of the World that these anarchists were crushed as never before, suffer from the neglect of the people, their employers, in other ways," the *Union* editorialized. Officers were required to pay attorneys to represent them in cases resulting from police work. The newspaper reported Stevens, who was shot, might leave the hospital crippled for life and unfit for duty because of an arm injury. If he should be forced to retire on half pay, the monthly pension would be $40 to $50.

The *Union* said subscriptions to start a police benevolent fund would be accepted at the newspaper office only on a voluntary basis, as police were forbidden to solicit "a single cent." The City Council unanimously endorsed this benefit fund.

In the first list of contributors the *Union* credited Spreckels with having given $500; Horace B. Day, president-treasurer of the Home Telephone Co., $25; State Senator Leroy A. Wright, $10; H. J. Otto and S. W. Hackett, citizens, $5 each; City Treasurer Don Stewart, $2; Harbor Engineer E. M. Capps, City Clerk Allen W. Wright, and a number of others, $1 each.

From this modest beginning the police relief fund of 1912 grew over the years to the present powerful San Diego Police Officers Association (SDPOA), which has been responsible for winning many benefits for officers. After the initial drive for funds, the City Council made membership in the relief association, organized July 28, 1912, obligatory for all police officers. The first officers of the new association were Detective Capt. Joseph E. Myers, president; Detective Inspector Frank A. Wisler, vice president; Paul S. Connors, court bailiff and member of the force, secretary; and Patrol Sgt. William H. Wetherbee, treasurer.

One of the fund-raisers, the annual souvenir booklet, was first published in 1914, a slick-paper historical document. It was published with the approval of Chief Wilson and Admiral Henry N. Manney, USN, retired, the councilman/police superintendent who had succeeded Sehon in 1913 when the latter was defeated in his bid for re-election. It devoted a full page to the chief and included full pages of whiskered commanding officers glaring at the public, plus photos of groups in the ranks.

The foreword of this souvenir booklet declared: "Regret is expressed that publication of this souvenir should have been delayed." Thereby hangs a tale.

From 1914 to the early 1960s there was strong opposition among the ranks against solicitation of money either for tickets to the annual balls, or sale of advertising for the souvenirs. There was a feeling that merchants were being sandbagged to buy blocks of tickets when the man with the badge showed up to ask for a "little contribution."

In the summer of 1913 the newspapers were bulging with articles about attempts of the police relief group to raise money. Here is an example from the July 13, 1913, issue of the *San Diego Sun*:

"Chief of Police Keno Wilson is a very busy man—so busy in fact, that there are times when he does not know what his most trusted men are doing. Chief Wilson, to use Admiral Manney's own words, did not know that a carnival given under the auspices of the police at Fifth and Broadway was rotten. This carnival had been running several days, together with a disgusting hoochee-coochee show. The police were taking tick-ets at the door. They were raking off 20 per cent of the receipts for their relief association."

Whereupon Admiral Manney ordered the carnival closed.

The city editor of the *Sun* knew a good story, even if it was at the expense of the cops. "And there is another thing Chief Wilson, who is a very busy man, did not know," the *Sun* confided to its readers. "He didn't know Sgt. Wetherbee of the association was, through solicitations, accepting sub-scriptions from 'Social Clubs' for the police souvenir annual! He knew nothing of this until told about it by the newspaper-men, after the Commercial Club, one of the clubs that con-tributed $100, was raided on a charge of gambling."

Detective Captain Joseph E. Myers, president of the police association, finally got into the dispute. This kicked off headlines like these in the *Union* on July 19: "Wilson Declares Bitter War: Myers Is Against Chief in Fund Imbroglio," and "Unsavory Affair Must Be Probed."

Well, before they could settle the dust and shut up the newspapermen, the first souvenir booklet was "a little delayed." The lesson was so bitter the "annual" was not issued again until 1922.

But there was a similar embarrassment in 1927, when a newly hired newspaper reporter took on the job of collecting money for advertising and gambled it all away at Tijuana's Foreign Club. The 1927 annual was also "slightly delayed."

The story was told by the late Jerry MacMullen in 1978, as he remembered his days as a young police reporter for the *Tribune* from 1921 to 1927:

> They had a big scandal several years before over a police souvenir annual, and they swore up and down another would never be printed. Well, a new reporter for the *Sun* named Joe Jones (not his real name) came to me and said, "Look, why don't we get out an annual for the Police Department, we can make some dough and the Relief Association can make some, too." I told him the Relief Association wouldn't go for it, they got too burned a few years before. The next day Joe came back and said they agreed to let us get out an annual, and we started working on it. I was doing the writing and Joe went out to sell the advertising.
>
> One day Joe didn't come to work, called in sick, and then a patrol lieutenant, Kewpie Treleaven, came in the police press room and said, "I was down at the Foreign Club in Tijuana last night and your friend, Joe, was also there, playing $20 gold pieces, and can he do that on a reporter's pay?" I said he couldn't and we checked and found he had collected for a lot of advertising and there was no accounting for this money, and then we discovered Joe had forged the treasurer's signature on a couple of checks made out to the Relief Association, and this put the whole thing right over the fence.
>
> Kewpie and I went to Joe's downtown hotel, and when he didn't answer the phone, went up and got the bellboy to open the door. We finally woke Joe up, and he confessed. He went to the police station with us and we had a session with Captain

Paul Hayes, the chief of detectives. When Joe was asked if he had been in the city before, he said he was a year before. They quickly checked the Identification Bureau and found Joe's photo on a card which stated he had been arrested for investiga-tion of bunco, but had been released.

> By this time the group had been joined by a deputy dis-trict attorney who said it was an open and shut case and Joe could be charged with forgery, if nothing else. But, the D. A. man said, police had to consider that if they signed a complaint it would bring a lot of scandal down on the department, because you hired a guy to sell advertising and didn't check your own files, where he had a questionable record. The D. A.'s sugges-tion was to put Joe on the afternoon train for Los Angeles with his solemn promise not to return. The cops quickly agreed, and then they all turned to me and said, "OK, Jerry, this guy was your partner, you got to finish up the police album and get us out of it."
>
> The *Union* reporter, Scotty McCloud, when I told him my problem, said to get in touch with an ex-policeman, a black officer named Reginald Townsend, who resigned after working as a detective. Cops were always quitting in those days for better jobs. I found Reginald and he and a partner went to work and came back with all kinds of advertising, they were the hardest workers I ever met up with. It was a good thing, Joe got away with a couple of thousand dollars.
>
> So I put in four months of the hardest work of my life and got the album together and to the printer. When it came out we had paid all our bills. The printer got $3,500, the Relief Association $1,100, and I something less than $300 for my efforts. It is a rather neat book but never would have happened if it hadn't been for Reginald Townsend and his fellow worker. I didn't know their method of getting advertising, didn't ever want to know, but they were very effective and they bailed us all out of a bad situation. I was sure then it would be the very last police souvenir annual that would ever be printed.

Many copies of this 1927 *Sixth Annual Souvenir Program* still exist, some in excellent condition, all highly prized by the surviving retired officers who were on duty the year it was issued.

The annual fund-raising police balls continued for fifty years, ending in 1960. Souvenir booklets were issued for the balls and advertising in the booklets was sold. These booklets were minor efforts, however, compared to the 1927 souvenir program.

Forty-four years were to pass before another "annual com-memorative album" was issued (in 1981 during the adminis-tration of Chief William Kolender). The 1981 album was a professional publication, a credit to any police department. Five years later a 1986 commemorative album was published in 1987. Both of these were 9 inches by 12, hardback, and printed on high-quality enamel paper. They were produced by a national publisher of such books, and neither carried any paid advertising.

A ghost of the past was present in this press release on

Most of the equipment of the San Diego police in 1908 is lined up in front of the police station at 1026 Second Street. The big man in the center with the long coat and bow tie is Harry von Den Berg, the first detective.

February 8, 1974, quoting Chief Ray L. Hoobler: "Numerous inquiries have been received concerning requests from various organizations to buy tickets, proceeds of which will benefit policemen or their programs. The department is not soliciting funds for any reason. Chief Hoobler said we long since have abandoned such things as the traditional Policeman's Ball or circuses because we thought them unprofessional. The Police Officers Association has also abandoned fund-raising events and does not sponsor drives for funds, in any manner whatsoever."

Former Chief Wes Sharp was a member of the Relief Association's board of directors when it nearly went bankrupt in the early 1930s, because so many members were in arrears in payment of dues, the main source of funding. There was no money even to pay a death benefit. Payroll deduction had been opposed by the city. "I went to John Peterson about 1934, during his second term as chief, and told him of our desperate need of collecting dues, and we had to have payroll deduction to collect them," Sharp said in 1987. "He was a good friend of mine and realized our dilemma, and managed to get us payroll deduction, which saved our skin."

Up until the early 1960s, the Relief Association (changed to the SDPOA in 1953 when it became incorporated) was supported by dues, proceeds of the annual police ball, and sale of advertisements in the souvenir booklets issued for the balls. The association now is supported by a monthly percentage of officer-member salaries and by investments. Every sworn

rookie officer is given a choice of becoming a member, and most of them sign up. Retirement, death, and disability benefits are paid by the city under terms of its agreements with the association. The association provides other benefits to the officers and their families.

A major police benefit was realized in 1910 only a year after being proposed by Capt. Sehon—retirement of officers at half pay. But the city had to do it the hard way.

Frank Northern, a Civil War veteran, joined the force in 1887. Everyone called him "Dad." He was the first to retire at half pay, $55 a month, early in 1911, after serving a suspension of four months.

"Dad" Northern had been relieved of duty as a headquarters "graveyard" desk sergeant early in September 1910 by Sehon. The police superintendent later released a letter to the City Council in which he charged the sergeant with sleeping on duty during his 11 p.m. to 8 a. m. shift, drinking beer with a visiting bartender and with junior officers at the station after midnight, and neglect of duty by leaving the station while on duty at 5 a.m. to take a walk around the block.

Northern promptly filed a request for a council hearing, his only recourse in those days, and told the newspapers he had never been reprimanded in more than twenty-two years on duty. The council, after holding lengthy hearings, upheld Sehon's charges but said Northern, after serving the four-month suspension, could retire. Old "Dad" took his suspension like the man he was, but he made another point to

The entire police force of 1897 appears in this lithograph from a booklet called "Souvenir of San Diego City." The men are, top row from left: Thomas Brodnax, Frank "Dad" Northern, William Warner, George Pringle. Second row: Bartholomew Moriarty, Chief James Russell, Robert Johnson. Third row: Thomas Blackledge, Frank McCarty, J. E. Harris, Edward Jones. Bottom row: George Couts, Sgt. Jóse Cota, George Cooley.

The record in years of drawing a retirement check was set by Lt. George W. Churchman, who joined the department January 15, 1912, and retired twenty years later in May 1932. He drew a retirement check until his death in November 1984, a total of fifty-two years. In an interview shortly before he died at age ninety-five, Churchman commented: "Even if I retired as a lieutenant, the retirement pay was only fixed at half all those years, and $75 a month in the 1980s doesn't go very far."

Many administrators have contributed to building the Police Officers Association to its strength in modern times, but it wasn't easy. An excellent example was the building in 1970 of its office at the corner of Kettner Boulevard and Market Street, across from the 1939 police headquarters. To conserve funds, many officers with building skills contributed their time. In recent years this office building was remodeled and enlarged to serve the ever-growing membership.

Because the POA represents officers as their collective bargaining agent in negotiating contracts with the city for pay and benefits, many consider it a labor union. But POA leaders call it more of a benevolent society that has bonded the force tightly together since it was founded, supporting its members through times of joy and times of sorrow. Anthony L. "Skip" DiCerchio, for sixteen years chairman of the POA negotiations team, said, "The rank and file of our members believe, because the directors and officers of the POA are full-time policemen representing full-time officers, this takes us out of the category of a labor union."

Only once in its history has the POA been represented by a labor union, when the Teamsters Union was contracted with in 1975. This was bitterly contested and soon the agreement was nullified. Many executives of the Police Department through the years have been elected by their peers and have served as officers of the SDPOA before taking top jobs in the department, including many chiefs.

the press: "Retirement also means that there will be other officers who will be benefited. I understand the pension law will be drafted into an ordinance before expiration of four months."

The Legislature in 1889 had passed a law providing for police pensions, but the city of San Diego had not followed up with an ordinance to conform. Northern, in getting his retirement the hard way, forced the city to conform, and an ordinance was passed as he predicted. This also opened the way for widows of officers killed in the line of duty to draw a pension of $27.77 a month. He insisted to the end he did nothing while on duty that had not been customary among officers for years, and his walks at 5 a.m. were to keep him from dozing on the job. He said he always called in another officer to take the desk duty while he sauntered around the block.

Northern had the last laugh. Old "Dad" was sixty-seven when he retired. He celebrated his ninety-sixth birthday in July 1940, and died in San Diego on January 17, 1941, thirty years after he began to draw the city pension of $600 a year.

Chapter 8
FAREWELL, STINGAREE

In the fall of 1909 a *San Diego Sun* newspaper article on the Stingaree pointed out that the red-light district "is not what it used to be."

"The district is there, and it's going to remain there, for the new administration doesn't want to break it up and spread it all over town," this story explained. "But the 'temperance saloons,' which run without license, are not selling alcoholic liquor when you wink to the bartenders, and the dance halls aren't what they used to be. What is more, it is likely that the dance halls and resorts of that sort will be put out of business." The sentence was prophetic.

The *Sun* continued:

This condition of affairs has been brought about by Captain John L. Sehon, superintendent of police, Chief of Police Wilson, and City Prosecutor Edgar Luce. Chief Wilson, Prosecutor Luce, Detective Smith, and a *Sun* reporter went through the district last night on a tour of inspection. The start was made at ten o'clock. Wilson is well known in that part of the city, where so much of his work lies, and when it got about that the chief was in the neighborhood with a detective and two strangers, there was no little commotion. Inhabitants of the district peered cautiously from windows and peeped like frightened rabbits from half-open doors, while others scurried around corners in quest of refuge.

The Legal Tender, one of the dance halls, was visited. This place is said to be conducted by Ed Reyes, proprietor of the Waldorf saloon on uptown Sixth Street, and was the only one of the dance halls where a government license was found exposed. In this establishment and in the eight other cheap dance halls Mr. Luce forced the bartenders to open fresh bottles of the stuff they are selling as a substitute for beer, and with the newspaper man he tasted it. It certainly was not beer. Mr. Luce took it for granted that a man couldn't get a jag on it.

While looking over things in the Pacific Squadron, another dance hall, Luce saw a boy apparently not over 16.

Worst of all about the dance halls and "temperance saloons"—and there was nothing good—was the presence of boys. After visiting the Yankee Doodle, the Little Casino, the Green Light, the Teagle, the Queen, the Legal Tender, the Pacific Squadron and the Reliance, the latter place being particularly popular with young boys, Luce said he may see fit to close up the dance halls or so-called temperance saloons in the very near future.

"These dance halls are the worst thing in the district," Luce said. "It is not my idea entirely to destroy the Stingaree and force its inmates all over the city, as I consider it is best to district them, but there is no reason these dance halls should run. I believe it will finally be necessary to shut up these temperance saloons and confine the women to less public quarters."

Walter Bellon, the city health inspector credited by historians with the main thrust that cleaned up the Stingaree and the old waterfront, in his memoirs designated for the Health Department a twelve-block area as the "Stingaree," from First to Fifth Street and from Market to K Street.

It took three years after the reform movement slate was elected before civic piety accomplished cleanup of Stingaree Town. Piety had to wait until the IWW troubles were taken care of.

In 1910–1911 there were newspaper stories of many fusses stirred up by the reform administration (demands to clean up the restricted district), but business continued as usual. The *Union* on September 29, 1910, reported Chief Wilson had ordered four women operating outside the district to leave town. The policy of the cops throughout the years again was summed up by Keno: "If immoral women come to San Diego believing they can live outside of the district, they will discover their mistake. I and all other members of the department are determined to keep such women in the district allowed to them."

By 1912 it was estimated at least one hundred of the shady ladies were operating in the Stingaree, in parlor or rooming houses and even in the old relics, the cribs and bullpens, compounds of bedrooms facing on a courtyard.

After the IWW disorders were settled, the civic purity problem was again raised by a Vice Suppression Committee headed by ministers and prominent women. Also known as the Purity League, this coalition raised the question, if the Stingaree was to continue, what image would the city leave with visitors to the forthcoming 1915 Panama-California Exposition? The days of police and city officials looking the other way (some were certain this attitude was fostered by owners of the Stingaree property) was coming to an end.

The *Union* on October 2, 1912, reported the Purity League was insisting police "slam the lid on the Stingaree." Police were still contending everything was under control.

Capt. Sehon, being a good politician, finally caved in to their demands, and ordered Wilson to close the district. The rowdy, wicked, colorful Stingaree was aroused on Sunday

morning, November 10, 1912, by messenger boys warning of imminent police raids, but the madams and their women had heard this many times before, and they stayed put.

Wilson mustered more than thirty policemen for the sweep, including every detective on the force. Before the raiding squads were sent into the district, all entrances and exits to the crib-yards and bawdy houses were blocked. No one was permitted to enter or to leave.

Not a single "john" was taken into custody. Prostitution in those days was strictly a female crime. The Oasis at 417 Fourth Street was the first place of call, and the police squad was followed by a crowd of onlookers. The next morning the *Union* thundered in headlines: "138 Women Are Arrested in Stingaree Raid," and in smaller type, "136 Promise to Leave City, Two Agree to Reform." In general the women treated the roundup as a joke. After they complained they were pinched before they had breakfast, police served them coffee and ham sandwiches.

Questioning continued at the Second Street police station from 10 a.m. to 6:45 p.m., with federal immigration officers participating. Six women were held for immigration processing. Two women said they would reform and were released to Purity League officials. The rest were told to go home, pack their bags, and be in Judge George Puterbaugh's justice court Monday morning. They complied. He fined each $100, suspended on condition she left town that afternoon.

An enterprising news reporter collared the ticket

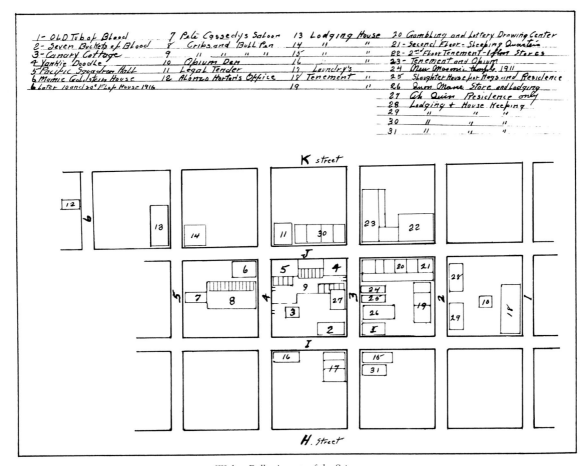

Walter Bellon's map of the Stingaree.

agent at the railroad station and quoted him as saying that he was doing a brisk business, but most of the ducats were round-trip. How many women really came back never was tabulated, but Chief Wilson told the press the fact only two of the fallen women wanted to reform was proof they had no desire to be saved. Assigning six detectives to check on the expected next moves of the women, he said that the force would do its best to prevent them from spreading to other parts of town, but that other cities had found that impossible.

The Stingaree girls drifted back and scattered over the town, as Keno had predicted. There were complaints that the brazen women were soliciting in the better parts of the city and that respectable housewives were being insulted by being accosted on the streets. As the girls of the night moved uptown, a reporter of the *Union* told readers that Chief Wilson and members of the force were entitled to a horse laugh.

But the police raids crippled the old Stingaree, and after the City Health Department successfully eradicated substandard housing, neglect settled in. Prostitution had been the mainstay of the economy, and many businesses closed. Sailors

who had that very year voted San Diego the "most popular liberty port on the West Coast" the next year picked San Francisco.

As police approached their one hundredth anniversary in the 1980s, the only evidence left of the old Stingaree was in expensively restored old hotels, one with a dining room named after Madame Ida Bailey. She had ruled over the young ladies of the Canary Cottage at 530 Fourth Street, a neat little story-and-a-half house, yellow with white trim, flanked by two huge rubber trees and nestling behind its white picket fence, the fanciest of all the temples of sin in its day.

The oldest retired cop strolling down lower Fifth Avenue might have heard echoes of the discordant sounds and drunken voices and thought a painted lady was peering out of an upstairs window, but it would be only in his imagination.

The Stingaree's history went back to 1887, when Alonzo Horton built his wharf at the foot of Fifth and thus began the development of San Diego's New Town. Now it has been overwhelmed by urban renewal, and sailors of the fleet seeking shady ladies look elsewhere.

Chapter 9
KENO'S DOWNFALL

A s noted earlier, gradual motorization of the force commenced in 1911. It culminated in 1916 with the stabling of all patrol horses and patrolmen driving their private cars in residential patrol areas. The officers were paid for the use of their automobiles. Foot patrol continued in the congested downtown area. For emergencies, motorcycle officers and detectives using autos were stationed at headquarters, waiting for calls. Sometimes it was necessary to send a foot patrolman on a streetcar with instructions to pick up another walking officer, if he could find one, on the way to an incident. The backbone of patrol, the horse, was gone, to return later for special purposes.

Control of motorized traffic became a problem as early as 1909, when H. E. Hill was hired as a motorcycle patrolman, furnishing his own bike. From this small beginning the traffic division grew rapidly over the years into one of the most important units of the force. The "Iron Horsemen," as cycle officers were called, became an elite unit.

Chief Wilson soon discovered the motor age could pile up unexpected expenses in addition to gasoline, oil, and maintenance—he had to hire people to drive the autos, and in 1911, when the department bought a Dodge touring car for $2,050, he paid out $99 for chauffeurs. Costs for autos increased yearly. By 1916 the department employed six chauffeurs, each paid $900 a year.

By 1916 the total value of the four autos in the police fleet—a Cadillac used for ambulance and paddy wagon service, another Cadillac, the 1911 Dodge touring car, and an Overland touring car—was $4,025.

The first machinist hired to take care of the fleet appears in the 1914 roster. He was C. H. Martin, who was paid $1,200 annually. After a few years, he was replaced by Henry Holland, who served more than forty years and retired as garage superintendent.

Back in 1905 San Diego had recorded the first traffic death from an automobile, Mrs. W. Adelaide Preston, sixty-three. She died from injuries suffered in a collision of her bicycle with an auto at Fifth and H (Market) streets.

Keno Wilson was reappointed to a third term of two years on May 8, 1913. By then he was chief of a department of eighty-seven persons. The force consisted of six divisions: patrol, detective, traffic, jail, identification bureau, emergency hospital and surgeon, and executive. From the 1907 beginning the detective division had grown from one man to a captain and ten inspector-detectives.

The force was saddened on May 18, 1913, by the death of Captain John Sehon, from Bright's disease and complications. He had been defeated earlier that year when he sought re-election to the City Council. An all-out effort was made to defeat him by the critics of his role in the IWW affair (including prominent men like the publisher E. W. Scripps, the merchant George W. Marston and the land developer Ed Fletcher), and they were successful. Sehon was buried with impressive ceremonies, and Keno Wilson in his eulogy said Sehon lived an honest and brave life.

Meanwhile, the problem of contacting a policeman walking a beat was solved with another of the new inventions, an electric call system. Headquarters was equipped with a Gamewell police alarm network, consisting of one hundred miles of copper wire, telephone call boxes at strategic corners, red lights strung in the middle of downtown intersections, five signal bells, and a control panel at the station. This cost $16,000, a sizeable amount in those days. A man walking on the beat could be notified to phone the station via the call box when the red light was turned on flashing from the station.

The Ocean Beach Wonderland Amusement Park opened on July 4, 1913, on an eight-acre site on the north side of Voltaire Street from Abbott Street to the sea, drawing crowds and creating some problems for police. This park revived the old popularity of Ocean Beach for weekend outings and eventually led to establishing a police substation on Abbott Street.

Admiral H. N. Manney, retired from the Navy and newly elected as councilman, was appointed police superintendent to succeed Sehon. A year later Manney ordered a new manual of police rules and regulations. The old one had not been revised in seventeen years. Under Rule Two of the new book, members of the force were forbidden to take presents, bestow testimonials, collect or receive money or anything else from citizens or others, circulate subscription papers or books, or sell tickets for any purpose. Rule Three prohibited promotion of any policeman who could not write a good official letter or report, "no matter how exemplary his conduct might be."

Previously, matrons in the City Jail had served as counselors and juvenile officers, but the new manual mentions for the first time a juvenile bureau: "There may be maintained a probation and juvenile bureau, and the chief of police may detail a patrolman to duty as a juvenile officer."

The old-style helmets were replaced with natty, black-

Here is the San Diego Police Department in 1914, assembled in Pantoja or New Town Park. Chief Keno Wilson is in the second row at the far right, seated on a horse as one of the mounted squad–where he is most comfortable. The elite of the force–the detectives–are in the two touring cars, one a Model T Ford, the other a Reo. The two women in one of the cars are the regular matron and her substitute. This is not the entire force, about twenty officers were busy keeping the peace elsewhere in the city.

visored caps. Uniforms were still blue.

The conflict in Europe to be known as World War I was far away from San Diego when the Panama-California Exposition opened on January 1, 1915, with a special police detail headed by Chief Wilson. Among the visiting dignitaries was Franklin D. Roosevelt, assistant secretary of the Navy. San Diego police did not have responsibility for keeping the peace inside the 1915 fair. This was assigned to the Pinkerton Detective Agency's guard division. These private guards wore uniforms of light blue patterned after those of the Spanish infantry.

But the police were responsible for keeping downtown safe and respectable during the Exposition. After the 1912 cleanup of the Stingaree, Chinatown remained a problem. It was a four-block area in the southwest corner of the Stingaree district, between First and Third and Island and K streets, and it was occupied almost entirely by Chinese stores, gambling houses, opium dens, and homes. A dark and gloomy place at night, it had only two principal streets, on which Chinese shacks fronted. The *Sun* described it thus:

In front of many of these places stands a sphinx-like celestial on guard at the door. When the police or a suspicious stranger approaches, the skulking yellow figure pulls a string that sounds the warning to the inner rooms and several doors are locked.

The police are certain the Mongolians are engaged in playing their favorite fan-tan game (cards or beans could be used) and Chinese dominoes, and that some are smoking opium and holding nightly revel but since it is done among themselves with little harm to the white man and with no disturbance, no attempt is made to force the doors and break up the doings within.

There are 14 different lottery companies operating in San Diego, and every dealer sells tickets to each company. Tickets are played from 10 cents up.

As the newspaper explained, very little attention had been paid to what the Chinese did among themselves. But on the afternoon of August 16, 1915, with the Exposition going full swing, police launched cleanup moves, raiding four of the biggest fan-tan houses in Chinatown. City Health Officer

Walter Bellon, architect of the 1912 police sweeps against prostitution in the Stingaree, commented on this move for city betterment:

Keno Wilson watched every move our [health] department made and decided to strike. He started on the several rooming houses, hotels, and along the waterfront, where he gathered up several dozen Negro and white women. Small raids continued all over the city until it was thought gambling, narcotics and flagrant prostitution were well controlled. Several Chinamen and a few Americans avoided arrest by escaping through the many back alleys. For this raid police were provided with heavy axes and jacks for breaking down heavy doors. Most of the entrances leading to the gambling halls on J Street were provided with doors three and four inches thick in double pattern. When the lookout spotted a stranger approaching, he would pull their latch string and enter, then both heavy doors would be locked by heavy cross bars, and nothing short of dynamite would break the doors down in time for police to make an arrest.

Security at the 1915 Panama-California Exposition in Balboa Park was handled by a body of men known as the "Balboa Guards." They were employees of the Pinkerton Agency, and wore distinctive uniforms of light blue, patterned after the uniform of Spanish infantry, conforming to the Spanish features of the Exposition. Besides the uniformed guard, one shown here with an admirer, Pinkerton detectives in civilian dress mingled with the crowds.

who had taken the vigilantes' side, had already been defeated for re-election. Now Keno also would suffer retribution.

A popular San Diego city manager, R. W. Flack, once said a manager's work should be measured by comparing the administration before he arrives with the administration that he leaves. This certainly is a fair way to judge the more than seven years Keno Wilson was chief of police. When he assumed command, the department had fewer than forty officers; when he was forced to relinquish control, the roster had grown to 103. He encouraged use of scientific methods. Police and other city employees received the protection of a civil service commission through an amendment to the city charter in 1915. A police relief association had been founded and was firmly entrenched. Transportation and communications had been modernized. An identification bureau, juvenile bureau, and medical department—with a police headquarters emergency hospital and ambulance—had been founded. In short, great strides had been made under Chief Wilson.

The Chinatown raid was Keno's last big operation. He had jumped from mounted patrolman to chief in 1909 and by the middle of 1915 had weathered three administrations and received reappointment from all of them. But by 1916, as he completed his seventh year as chief, the political winds were blowing the wrong way for him. He had only eight months and eight days left to command. His role in the IWW troubles had been greatly praised at the time but some who had urged him on may have had second thoughts later and blamed him for their embarrassment. The episode left a lasting residue of anger among the defenders of free speech. They did not forgive or forget. The vigilantes had remained anonymous but Keno was highly visible. Sehon and Dist. Atty. Harold Utley,

Edwin Capps was elected mayor again in 1915. He had served in the mayor's office for a term in 1899–1901 and then had become the city engineer. Now back in power, Capps wanted to keep Keno as chief for two more years. The council balked at confirming reappointment and became hopelessly deadlocked. Wilson held on to his office, protected by law. The press kept asking who was chief of police? Finally, in January 1917 the state District Court of Appeal in Los Angeles ordered Mayor Capps to appoint a police chief within five days: the council had won a mandamus suit against the mayor.

Bowing to the court order, the mayor sent his appointment to the council January 6, 1917. His choice was J. E. Steer, formerly of Iowa and then living on Grant Hill in San

Above: Two of the police chiefs who followed J. Keno Wilson in the office: Steward P. McMullen, who led the force during World War I, and Joseph Steer, whose lack of experience as a lawman was a handicap. Right: Crime Report of 1917.

CRIMES OF PERSONS EXAMINED

	Jan.	Feb.	Mar.	April	May	June	July	Aug.	Sep.	Oct.	Nov.	Dec.
Adultery		1										
Alien Enemy							1					
Assault D. Weapon			1			1		2		2		
Assault to Murder			2				1					
Battery			1				1	3		1		
Begging	1											
Bunco	1								3			
Burglary	7	1	1	1	4	11	3	5	2	8	4	2
Carrying C. Weapons				1			1	1		1		2
Defraud Inkeeper	1											
Dis. the Peace											3	3
Drunk											1	
Fictitious Checks	1	3	2	2	3		4		1	4	3	
Forgery	1		2	3				1		1		
Felony Embezzlement							1		1		1	
Fornication												1
Grand Larceny	1	4	3	8	7	5	5	2		1	6	2
Homicide											1	
Impersonating Officer					1							
Insanity							1					
Inj. Public Jail			1									
Lewd and Lasc. Acts	1						2		1		1	
Manslaughter						1						
Murder						1			3			
Obtaining Money F. P.				1								
Obtaining Property F. P.					3							
Opiates in Poss.	6	3	2			1	4	2	1	1		2
Petit Larceny	10	9	4	4	3	2	3	5	8	4	5	9
Perjury									1			
Parole Violator					1							
Pimping	3						1					
Pickpocket	1	2				4	1					3
Rape						1			2	1		1
Robbery	4	1	5	1	7	1	1	6	6	4	3	8
Sell. Liq. to Soldiers							4	5				3
Slacker									1	1		
Sell. Gov. Property												1
Smuggling	2	4	7		3	4	3	2	6	1	4	
Use Mail to Defraud						1						
Vagrancy	5	1	5	2	1	1	1	1	3		1	4
Vagrancy Lewd.	2	1			3	4						
Viol. Probation							1					
Witness	1										1	
White Slavery						2						
	48	30	36	27	37	47	37	30	40	33	35	41

OCCUPATION OF PERSONS EXAMINED

	Jan.	Feb.	Mar.	April	May	June	July	Aug.	Sep.	Oct.	Nov.	Dec.
Accountant	1											
Baker					1	1		1				
Barber			1				1	1				
Bartender				1	1		1	2	1			
Bell-Boy				1	1		1	1			1	1
Blacksmith							1					
Bookkeeper												
Boilermaker		1										
Bootblack			2							1		
Broker										1		1
Butcher						1				1		1
Buttermaker	1											
Carpenter	1			2	1			1	1	2	2	1
Cement Worker					1							
Cigar Maker										1	1	

Diego. The *Union* reported: "He (Steer) has lived in San Diego about fourteen years. He says he does not think the fact he has not had any police experience will handicap him." Steer was reported to be fifty years of age, but didn't look it. Short and stocky, with black hair, mustache, and eyes, he had been a member of several grand juries and was said to be a man of considerable wealth.

The *Union* on the morning of January 11 said council members were ready to confirm Steer as chief. "It has been arranged to give J. Keno Wilson a minor position on the force to tide him over until such time, less than two years hence, when he is entitled to a police pension," the newspaper reported. Wilson told reporters he was glad it was all over. His future on the force was indeed shaky. He had advanced from patrolman to police chief, but some now said he could not again hold a police position.

Steer was confirmed, made his bond, and became chief on January 11. On January 17 Steer made Keno an acting sergeant, a job he lost when Steer was fired.

In the spring of 1917, Louis J. Wilde was elected mayor, along with three new city councilmen, and Capps was out of office. Steer was removed by the City Council as incompetent after serving less than four months. The new chief, S. P. McMullen, reinstated Wilson as a patrolman, and thirteen months later another new chief, James Patrick, promoted Keno to sergeant. Patrick had been appointed to the force in 1912 by Wilson.

Keno Wilson in his sunset days on the Police Department was remembered as the desk sergeant, a one-man counterpart to the modern system of dispatching officers. A single telephone was his communication system. For emergencies, he would press a button which rang a bell in the alley behind the old Second Street station to alert the ambulance or paddy wagon crews, and then the emergency motorcycle rider or an officer in a car would be dispatched.

Wilson stuck to the desk job until May 27, 1926, when he retired with twenty-five years and six months of service. His pension was $25 monthly. Then he became a deputy U. S. marshal in charge of the San Diego office. Illness forced him to retire from active service in 1932. The old cowboy died at his home, 2103 Island Avenue, on September 24, 1934, ending an era.

Chapter 10
AN EXPERT OPINION

After Steer's ouster for incompetence, Mayor Louis Wilde postponed appointing a new police chief. On May 5, the day the mayor and new council took office, James Patrick, then second in command, was appointed acting chief and served for five months until the city fathers made up their minds.

The *Union* on May 6, 1917, reporting on the inaugural ceremonies, said there was "talk galore, but no definite action." Mayor Wilde did go on record as being unpledged and still uncertain about appointment of a chief, and he wanted time to decide whether the force should be completely reorganized. As a result of a conference, the City Council passed unanimously a resolution authorizing the mayor to contract for an expert to reorganize the Police Department and put it on an efficient and economical basis.

The officials refused to say who they had in mind to do the "reorganizing," but the *Union* reported that Chief of Police August Vollmer of Berkeley, famous for his work as a police administrator and well known in San Diego, would "get the call." (Chief Vollmer later was to become dean of police science at the University of California at Berkeley.)

The newspaper had the right information. Wilde hired Vollmer for a fee of $1,700, and the Berkeley chief arrived in San Diego on May 22, wasting no time to get at the job. He told the press: "I am not here for the benefit of the police, the council, or any group or individual. I am here for the benefit of the people."

In his report two weeks later, Vollmer thanked the people of San Diego for their courteous treatment and for assistance in collecting the data for the report. He warned that his recommendations for reorganizing the force included some radical departures from established police methods. The "tried and true" methods of the existing system had failed, and other policies must be pursued in order to improve the San Diego Police Department to even a small degree.

As a person who has spent much of a lifetime delving into police science and methods, I cannot but be amazed by Vollmer's report. He devoted nine single-spaced typed pages to positive recommendations for reorganization and fourteen pages to outlines of courses for the police school, which was one of his musts for reorganization. "The department may be divided for this purpose [schooling] into two separate classes, each class to attend three lectures or laboratory demonstrations each week," the report stated. "Instructors may be

obtained among the professional men and women of San Diego, who I am sure will readily volunteer their time and services for the good of the cause."

The outline began with physics, followed by chemistry, biology, toxicology, anthropology, heredity, psychology, psychiatry, criminology (five pages), police organization and administration, methods and procedures, criminological microbiology and parasitology, police micro-analysis, public health, first aid to injured, and, lastly, law. The outline also touched on atomic and molecular hypotheses and on psychoses of pregnancy, menopause, arteriosclerosis, and puberty.

Vollmer condemned the jail and police headquarters, the first of many such public criticisms that twenty years later would lead to construction of new quarters and a larger, modern jail at 801 West Market Street.

Every officer in every rank agreed with this comment: "Competent officials can only be secured and retained by offering salaries which will attract desirable men and women, after they have qualified by passing the necessary examinations." He said all employees, other than the chief and records superintendent, should be paid $100 per month; at the end of two years of schooling, all patrolmen, clerks, and matrons should be paid $115. Sergeants, investigators, and inspectors should get $125 monthly. (The 1917 pay scale for police patrolmen was maximum $100 monthly, sergeants $115, and lieutenants $150.)

All this was too much, coming only two years after a city Civil Service Commission had replaced the comfortable old spoils system of hiring and firing. Vollmer drew general contempt from the brass and from the ranks of the force for his recommendation to cut manpower from 120 to 54. It had taken the department eight years to build its strength to 120, and now an outsider, in the interest of cutting costs, would arbitrarily slash the force by more than half.

The mayor and council ignored almost everything Vollmer suggested. Although schooling had been a cornerstone of the Vollmer report, it would be another thirty years before one of the essential requirements of a good police department—a police school—would be established. It would be almost another ten years before another suggestion to save money—installation of a telephone exchange connecting all police officers with a single number to call—would be adopted. Vollmer in his report maintained that "the present arrangement of many numbers is very confusing, unsatisfactory, and twice as expensive. Two home (private) phones are sufficient, one for the chief's office and the other for the sergeant's desk." (On October 31, 1926, a telephone exchange of the type he recommended was placed in operation, with the phone company switching over to Franklin 1101, the number to call police for any type of service. This number was used for more than a quarter of a century.)

Mayor Wilde and his council received and filed Vollmer's report, undoubtedly with some private comments, and then did what came naturally. James Patrick served as acting chief from May until October while the public thought the Vollmer report was being studied. Then the mayor nominated and the council confirmed Steward P. McMullen as police chief, effective October 9, 1917.

McMullen had been a resident of San Diego for about five years, coming here from the East. He had been for many years identified with the Cudahy Packing Company, establishing plants throughout the nation at which thousands of men were employed. One of the Cudahy plants was established here.

Police Chief James Patrick. He met the challenge as police chief, serving more than eight years with honor and political acumen.

April 6, two days before the election, in type big enough to grab readers: "Police and Gamblers." The ad purported to give the results of an investigation by two private detectives, hired by the mayor, into city vice conditions. These operatives listed by address and name the operators of twenty places where they asserted gambling was conducted when they visited.

Voters were soon informed that the mayor had demanded the resignation of the chief, and if Wilde was re-elected, McMullen would be fired. Wilde won the election of April 8, and McMullen promptly sent his resignation to the City Council, prompting newspapers to comment that he beat the mayor to the threat of dismissal. One councilman, Virgilio Bruschi, said McMullen was the best chief of police since the force was established. The council passed a resolution congratulating the chief on his administration. Councilman Bruschi, a grocer and political wheel, called attention to McMullen's "splendid" handling of law and order when the streets had filled with thousands of sailors and soldiers in training here during the war.

McMullen led the Police Department through the last year of World War I. In his 1917 annual report, McMullen said liquor traffic had not been a police problem until 1917, when San Diego became a military center, with Navy activity, mobilization of great numbers of men for all armed services, and construction of a big Army base on Linda Vista Mesa.

In the report McMullen also said he was not satisfied with the gambling situation, and had reason to believe bookmaking and other forms of gambling were running, principally in social clubs and cigar stores guarded with heavily locked doors and lookouts. Obtaining evidence was almost impossible.

Mayor Wilde's bid for re-election in 1919 soured his relationship with McMullen. A black headline ran across the top page of a political advertisement in the Sunday *Union* of

McMullen's political ambition came into bloom later. He was elected city councilman, served for four years, and then was elected county supervisor, serving for six years.

James Patrick, who had led the force for five months in 1917, again was named acting chief, and a month later was made permanent head of the department. He served as chief with honor (and political acumen) for eight years, a record for tenure of office until the administration of A. E. Jansen (1947–1962).

Chapter 11
THE ROARING TWENTIES

James Patrick took over a fairly well-functioning department and, to his credit, built it up as the city boomed. Twice he had been acting chief of police. Most important, he was a veteran who had joined the force in 1912, the IWW year, and had lived through the worst and finest hours of the department. His advancement was steady. He took command on April 9, 1919, less than seven years after joining the force.

Two problems occupied Patrick's administration. The first was manpower to police a city growing rapidly both in population and in square miles. The second was all-consuming—the challenge of staying in office. He walked these two tightropes very well, increasing the size of the department while setting a record for tenure in office—eight years and 110 days—that stood for nearly thirty years.

In San Diego they were the booming Twenties, with substantial building of all kinds. Downtown a skyline was created that would remain unchanged for nearly three decades. The federal census set the 1920 population at 74,683, and that nearly doubled by 1930 to 147,995. In the same decade San Diego County's population increased from 112,248 to 209,659.

Residential construction kept pace with downtown development. The city annexed East San Diego (an incorporated city) and housing subdivisions were developed along the ocean side of Point Loma and in Talmadge Park.

Ten Navy installations were built or authorized in the decade and San Diego was on its way to becoming a great Navy port. The installations included the Marine Corps Recruit Depot, the Naval Hospital in Balboa Park, and the Naval Training Center.

Streetcar lines to Ocean Beach and La Jolla were completed in 1924, the Mission Beach Amusement Center opened in 1925, and construction was started late in the decade on a new highway north through Rose Canyon. Registration of automobiles and trucks soared. In 1920 there were 18,000 such vehicles in San Diego County; by 1923 registrations had risen to 30,000.

Population growth, with expanding streetcar lines plus affordable autos and paved streets and roads, made living in the suburbs possible. San Diego spread over the mesas cut by its many canyons. The eastern boundary before annexation of the city of East San Diego in 1923 was, aptly, Boundary Street, which ran from the rim of Mission Valley almost to National City. After the annexation, residential tracts were built to the east. Money was plentiful after the initial recession following the end of World War I, and prosperity seemed to be lasting forever—until the big market crash in October 1929. The city had been decentralized, and the trend was set for each area to have its own trading center and neighborhood loyalty.

Files surviving in the office of the city clerk testify to the need for more officers. Reading these many letters from diverse groups throughout the city, urging support of the police, one speculates that either the public in those days needed no prodding to write letters to councilmen or Patrick was an excellent politician.

During the Roaring Twenties political observers agreed that no organization or individual boss controlled the election of mayors and council members in San Diego. Local elections were now nonpartisan, and, in the absence of political organizations, neighborhoods and other minor pressure groups exerted considerable influence. Patrick was aware of this and used these groups.

He had one boss, the mayor, who under powers given him by charter was in a position to direct police affairs. Patrick was appointed by Mayor Louis J. Wilde, who did not seek re-election when his term ended in 1921. The police chief was fortunate in the election of John L. Bacon to succeed Wilde as mayor: Bacon, an engineer, remained in office six years, and Patrick stayed on the job with Bacon's strong backing.

Patrick chose a low profile and cut through pettifoggery to make his administration stable, smooth, and effective. Patrick also knew the value of good publicity. Each year a neatly printed annual report was issued, and he encouraged the issuance of souvenir annuals by the Police Relief Association.

These annuals, carrying pictures of all personnel of the department with short historical summaries and articles about divisions, were issued in 1922, 1924, and 1925, with Patrick's blessing. Today they are historical documents. They informed the public about what its force was doing and improved the morale of the officers.

In the 1925 issue, historian Jerry MacMullen, then a young reporter covering the police for the *Tribune*, was a contributor:

> No subject is of greater interest than our present orgy of crime. The popular thing is to blame the Police Department. As a matter of fact, they are least to blame of any. The trouble is that police are trying to buck an unbeatable combination—

For fifty years (1920s to 1970s) San Diego offered police ambulance service off and on, expanding the fleet of emergency vehicles from only downtown assistance to outlying neighborhoods as substations were established. Oldtimers recall fondly "the old Grey Goose," a name given this converted Cadillac ambulance, shown with the civilian chauffeur and two patrolmen.

political influence and a system of legal procedure which is a crying disgrace to the country. The present relation between police and [criminal] law is one of "We catch 'em—you turn 'em loose." Easy probation and paroles, the indeterminate sentence law, and legal hocus-pocus are the principal monkey wrenches in the machinery of justice.

And Mayor Bacon in the same edition had this to say:

Police work is changing, becoming more complicated as the field widens, and it is fast rising to the dignity of a profession. We feel proud of the way the San Diego Police Department has met these ever-increasing responsibilities.

Faced with the fact that San Diego is a border city, a seaport, and a city which attracts all types of tourists and strangers during all seasons of the year, crime has been kept down to a remarkable degree. The public is slowly changing its attitude toward the policeman and realizing more and more what he stands for and what he is trying to do.

The police departments in many of our larger cities are seriously handicapped by politics and political influence, and it is a pleasure to be able to say that I believe that this great menace is having less and less influence on the San Diego Police Department every year.

In an interview with Patrick by *Tribune* reporter George Dissinger, published January 3, 1953, the former chief was described as quiet-spoken and reluctant to talk about himself.

"There is not much to report," Patrick said. "I just did my job. There was nothing outstanding about my work." His wife did not agree. She showed a letter from Mayor Walter Austin, written when Patrick retired from the force in 1932. In it the mayor said, "I find your record stands without blemish."

Patrick had joined the Army during the Spanish-American War and served a total of fourteen years, with duty in Puerto Rico, Cuba, the Philippines, and stateside. After he was married, he decided Army life was for single men. He bought his discharge (quite legal then), came to San Diego, and joined the force.

In his annual report for 1919, Patrick stressed the unrest of the period following the end of World War I and the demobilization of soldiers and sailors. Five days before Patrick became chief, Army Captain Herbert W. Meyers, representing the federal Fosdick Commission on Training Camp Activities, made strong charges before the City Council. The *Union* (May 15, 1919) gave front-page play to the captain's charge that San Diego cabarets were the "vilest" he had ever encountered, and the cheapest thing in town was the flesh of young girls. The charges brought a prompt and sharp denial from Mayor Wilde.

Puritanism was riding high in the nation. In 1918 a partial wartime Prohibition banned the distilling of hard liquor and reduced the alcoholic content of beer. No alcoholic beverages of any kind were to be served to men in uniform.

Above: Police reporters George O. Potts (Union), J. Wesley Hall (Sun), G.F. MacMullen (Evening Tribune). Right: Officer Thomas E. Remington, who joined the department on March 2, 1926, is shown in the police uniform worn from 1919 to 1935, olive drab, khaki doughboy style, with choker collar. Remington later was assigned to motorcycle patrol and retired as a sergeant.

Patrick submitted his annual report for 1919 in January 1920, just as the eighteenth Amendment was going into effect, providing for full Prohibition of liquor nationwide. The chief called attention to the marked difference the partial wartime Prohibition had already made on the number of drunken persons arrested. There were more than 1,000 in the first half of 1919 and not many more than 100 in the second half—"quite a material decrease." The legal liquor business was shutting down; the bootleg business was not yet underway.

The unsettled conditions by the end of World War I required extraordinary police service, Patrick said in his 1920 annual report. "Idlers, fakers, thieves, swindlers, and all classes of crooks were preying upon the public, and constant watching and ingenious methods had to be employed to prevent crime and apprehend offenders."

During his first year, Chief Patrick changed the

department uniform from the original blues to khaki with a choker collar, which was to remain in use until the blue uniform returned in 1934.

Motorized crooks became a problem about 1922, as this December 9, 1922, story in the *Sun* shows:

Chief Patrick announces, in order to compete with the motorized crooks of today, he is asking the City Council for funds for three automobile patrolmen to cover outlying residential districts during night hours.

These motorcar patrolmen are not to supplant the bicycle men or foot patrolmen, says the chief, but are in addition. Automobile-equipped officers can cover three times the territory a bicycle man can cover and are of untold value in chasing automobile bandits and thieves who escape in motor cars.

Chief Patrick does not intend that the Police Department buy autos. His idea is to have each automobile patrolman

In this picture from the 1925 souvenir album published by San Diego police, five members of the vice squad—called "Special Detail, Morals and Liquor"—sit on a bench outside the police station at 732 Second Street. The squad leader, Sgt. Robert P. Newsom, center, became police chief August. 1, 1932. Much of their duty was enforcement of the "dry" law. Right: These five officers comprised the bicycle squad of San Diego police in 1917. Left to right, Charles Harris, F.J. Slattery, Herb Webster, George Churchman, and Frank Connors. Harris was killed on duty in April 1927. Webster was disabled when shot patrolling in Point Loma. Slattery became a detective lieutenant, and Churchman, who retired in 1932 as a detective lieutenant, drew a pension for more than fifty years.

TO PROTECT AND SERVE

Above: San Diego Patrolman H. E. Hill (later detective sergeant), one of the first officers assigned to traffic duty in the late 1920s, is shown with his wife beside their Dodge touring car. Hill joined the force January 17, 1911. Below: These four men in 1922 manned a San Diego police ambulance. Left to right, Patrolman-driver George Smith, Paul P. Plaisted, Lewis Lusk, and George Wilson.

furnish his own car of whatever make or model he sees fit, as long as it is fast and a serviceable machine and [the patrolman] is given a monthly allowance for upkeep.

Chief Patrick in a speech on October 23, 1923, listed the strength of his force at 103 persons, including eleven detective sergeants and sixty-four patrolmen. He had a captain of detectives, a captain of police, one lieutenant of detectives, a lieutenant of police, and seven sergeants of police.

Annexation of East San Diego in 1923 had added to department strength. The East San Diego city marshal at the time of annexation, Nat McHorney, Jr., and two deputies, Ed Moore and H. W. Jack, were transferred to the San Diego force.

Problems for outlying patrol were increased midway in Patrick's term, when the sand dunes and mud flats of Mission Bay were opened to the public by completion in 1924 of an electric rail line to the beach areas. Part of Mission Beach became an all-year residential suburb.

The development of beach property to the north, spurred by the auto and by the expansion of the street rail system, led to establishing a second substation in La Jolla about 1921. The first "sub" at Ninth and University had been closed and the Ocean Beach station was redesignated No. 1. The La Jolla station became No. 2 and in 1923, with the annexation of East San Diego, the station there became No. 3.

Prohibition brought major problems to San Diego police in enforcing with federal agents this drastic measure. San Diego was on the front line of the battle between the dry law agents and the smugglers, bootleggers, and speakeasy operators. The problem locally was made acute by proximity to the Mexican border and by San Diego's being a port city. Alcohol from a Tijuana distillery and other liquors—many of top grade—that poured into the city by land and sea made bootlegging big business. Stills sprouted like dandelions.

The San Diego Police Department had two men whose training on the bunco squad made them perfect for enforcement of the dry laws.

Police ambulance in front of City Jail, 1922.

They were Detective Sergeants George Sears, later to become chief, and Richard Chadwick, who had become an officer in 1910 and eventually was promoted to detective. Chadwick honed his investigative skills preceding Prohibition when he was sent to the Ocean Beach substation to patrol an area which then was the "hot spot" of the city's night life, with five saloons and cabarets going full blast. More policemen were stationed there than in the central district.

Sears and Chadwick made a good team. They became known as the "Gold Dust Twins" in newspaper accounts of their raids and arrests. They were joined by Maurice (Mike) Shea, who was to become a detective sergeant. These three made most of the Prohibition enforcement headlines, as they assisted Charles Cass, a federal agent assigned from Los Angeles.

The dry laws were highly unpopular in San Diego. Throughout the United States the dry laws corrupted police departments, and stories persisted of payoffs here, but none are documented and no one from the local Police Department was brought to trial for bribery.

One story, published in the *Union* on June 1, 1927, summarizes the temptations faced by honest cops. Motorcycle Patrolman Jack Byers of the Chula Vista force chased an auto which ran a boulevard stop. As he walked to the auto to issue a citation, he noticed what later were counted as twenty-five one-gallon cans containing alcohol.

As Byers reached the car, one of the two occupants said, "Will $1,000 be enough?" It was said to be customary for an officer finding a liquor haul to be offered money if he would write a traffic ticket and let the smugglers go on their way. Byers was a different breed. He arrested the two in the car and seized the bootleg alky.

What makes this story more interesting is that the average policeman in 1927 made $100 a month, or $1,200 yearly. Byers turned down the equivalent of ten months' salary.

In the four years from 1923 to 1926, San Diego police seized 2,587 gallons of whiskey, 5,466 gallons of mash, and untold gallons of homemade wine. They smashed 177 liquor stills.

A turnover in city politics in 1927 led to Patrick's decision to step down, but not to leave the force. Mayor Bacon, whose support had kept Patrick in the chief's job, decided not to seek election, and Harry C. Clark, a lawyer, was elected mayor. A new council majority also took office, among them S. P. McMullen, the former chief of police.

Proud of holding the highest police office for the longest time, Patrick announced he was ready to turn over the reins to someone else. He reverted to his rating of lieutenant, but was given the title of assistant chief. That lasted only a couple of months. On May 31, 1927, his long service ended with retirement. Patrick made a bid for another public office, running for sheriff in 1934. In the primary election he ran fourth and last.

James Patrick lived quietly in retirement. During the forty-nine years he and his wife were San Diego residents, the last forty-six were spent at 3981 Front Street, his home when he died on January 16, 1960.

Patrick's administration, although far from flamboyant, ranks as one of the best in the history of the force. His Army training contributed to the discipline and loyalty of the force. His long tenure as chief helped Patrick mold the Police Department into a "family affair," at least in the opinion of Robert Newsom, Jr., a retired sheriff's inspector and son of Robert Newsom, chief in the 1930s. The son, describing himself as "one of the police brats," said the force was not only a family—it was a closed corporation.

When Patrick stepped down another era of stability ended. Troubled times were ahead, including the Great Depression.

Chapter 12
REVOLVING AGAIN: 1927-1934

If a master plan had been devised to disorganize the force, none would have worked better than to change chiefs at least once a year, and during the seven years from 1927 to 1934 the city fathers went that one better—they saddled the department with a new police chief on the average of every eleven months.

It was a time of transition. At the beginning, Prohibition remained in effect. By the end of this seven-year period, the nation was enjoying Repeal. At the beginning, political control of the Police Department continued much as it had been since 1889. At the end, a new City Charter had introduced a city manager system that took control of the Police Department away from the mayor and City Council and gave the appointment of the police chief to the city manager. At the beginning, there was no consistent city policy on enforcement of the laws against bootlegging, vice, and gambling. At the end, a move toward stricter enforcement had begun.

The first chief in this transitional series of eight police administrations was Joseph V. Doran, picked by Mayor Harry S. Clark to succeed Patrick on May 31, 1927.

Doran, a detective sergeant, was a handsome man of medium height and weight who carried himself well. He was known among colleagues as a "good politician." As a young man he had served in the Army's 6th Field Artillery, seeing considerable duty along the Texas border. After serving a temporary period on the Police Department during the 1915 Exposition, he was appointed to the force in 1917. A volunteer, he served in World War I and then returned to police duty, becoming a detective in mid-1919. Fellow officers liked Doran and said he was fearless and an excellent investigator.

Patrick, meanwhile, reverted to his permanent rank of lieutenant. Doran put him in command of the East San Diego substation, but Patrick quickly chose retirement in preference to continued service as a subordinate officer. Capt. Arthur Hill was put in charge of the patrol division and Capt. Paul Hayes named chief of detectives.

In the detective bureau, the office he knew best, Doran made substantial changes. He established all-night detective service. He broke up the "purity" squad, another name for the vice squad, and used the men for more urgent investigations. He assigned Officer Hugh Rochefort, later to be a detective sergeant, to assist Charles Cass, the federal Prohibition agent here, and agreed to take small liquor cases into city courts and let the Federal agents prosecute the larger ones.

Doran made a change in a tradition on the detective squad, where officers had worked singly on a case. Doran believed better work would be done by detectives working in pairs.

By the time Doran became chief, the lifeguard unit, then under the Police Department, was adding men as the use of city beaches expanded. The 1927 roster shows two police lifeguards, Calvin Burns, captain of guards, and A. K. Kraus. Both were stationed at Ocean Beach. Seasonal guards were added during the summer.

The city Civil Service Commission was attracting more qualified men as recruits. And fingerprinting of applicants was a godsend to police, as a Los Angeles report showed. In 1924, the first year the Los Angeles Police Department training school operated, fingerprints revealed that 17 out of 154 recruits accepted had arrest records, and some had applied under fictitious names. One had been arrested in Illinois for murder, others were burglars, holdup men, or rapists. Out of the second class, nine were found to be convicts. But in the third class, only one recruit had a criminal record: the news about fingerprint identification traveled fast.

Doran, together with Arthur Hill, established the traffic bureau after deaths and injuries in accidents soared. Capt. Hill, No. 2 man in the department, was put in charge of the new bureau, with six motorcycle officers. Within a year this squad was increased to thirteen officers, with orders to ticket at least one driver in every accident. The system worked. The accident rate was reduced.

When Doran's two-year term expired, on May 11, 1929, Mayor Clark picked Capt. Hill, fifty-five, to be chief. He refused to give the press a reason for dumping Doran, and under the charter at that time, no reason was needed. Doran resumed his permanent rank of detective sergeant, and later became a patrol captain.

Hill, who joined the department January 21, 1914, made sergeant in three years, and in six years was a captain. Hill came from a pioneer family in the El Cajon Valley, where he rode horseback seven miles to a valley school. He came to San Diego around 1891, remembering a city then of around fifteen thousand residents, no sidewalks, no pavement, and plenty of mud or dust in the streets.

Before he became a San Diego policeman, Hill was an actor and playwright throughout the West and a gold and copper miner in Arizona. His father, Ben P. Hill, was San Diego

Joseph V. Doran. Handsome, fearless, good investigator, he established the first all-night detective service in two years as chief, 1927 to 1929.

Arthur R. Hill. Actor turned lawman, noted for solving gangster-type murder robbery of Caliente race track car. Led the force from mid-1929 to 1931.

Lieut. George Churchman. Shown receiving police department plaque at ninetieth birthday party in 1979, joined force in 1912, retired in 1932, drawing pension for over fifty years.

County sheriff from 1892 to 1894. After joining the force, Arthur Hill met Ida Griffin, the widow whom Keno Wilson had appointed as the first full-time police matron, and they were married in 1919.

Within two weeks after becoming chief, he was leading the manhunt for the machine-gun killers of two guards on the Agua Caliente (Mexican gambling resort) money car. This seemed to be "big-time" crime and the first here in which machine guns were used, although they were common during Prohibition back East. The Caliente heist on May 20, 1929, had been set up by a bootlegger, who figured it would net $100,000, two days' take from the resort. The big money shipment was actually scheduled the day after the holdup. The crime netted only $5,500 in cash and $60 in checks.

Two men in a new Ford coupé without a windshield had pulled up behind the northbound money car, a Cadillac, on old Highway 101, on the dike just north of National City. The robbers opened fire with machine guns, shooting out the tires and stopping the Cadillac. The two Mexican guards in the Cadillac, who were taking the money to a San Diego bank, blasted back with their pistols, but both were killed and the Cadillac was riddled with bullet holes.

The murder-robbery set off a massive manhunt. The police must have received a tip which led to the capture of one suspect, Marty Colson, in bed in the apartment of a bootlegger friend near Balboa Park. Colson had been wounded in the shoulder by a slug from his companion's machine gun. The other robber, Lee Cochran, was arrested by Los Angeles police in the apartment of a friend in Los Angeles, again as a

result of information received by police. The robbers were found guilty and sentenced to life in state prison. One committed suicide in prison; the other was paroled in 1942. It turned out they had no big-time gang connection, although they used the racketeers' weapon of choice.

The newspapers had a field day with this case, and it made the new chief look good, but the next year he was exposed to less favorable news coverage: the City Council filed charges against him on March 10, 1930. Mayor Clark believed the charges were an outgrowth of a liquor case the summer before. Lieutenant George Churchman recalled this case in a 1980 interview:

> I was head of the vice squad that summer of 1929 when we had a veterans' organization convention in the city. The head of the sheriff's vice squad took his vacation during the period, and I was sorry I didn't take mine. Right in the middle of that convention, Officer Mike Shea, working on the squad, told me the conventioneers were buying liquor openly at a spot uptown, right over the counter. I took a squad of men and knocked off the place, confiscating the liquor, claimed to be worth $17,000.
>
> In a little while Chief Hill came roaring in and wanted to know what the hell was going on. Then the city fathers wanted the liquor given back to the source. I told them the booze had been turned over to federal authorities, and that ended that.

An ouster petition eventually was filed against Hill. The mayor said two grand juries investigated the liquor case and didn't find anything illegal. "Nothing came of the charges," Churchman said, "except a lot of newspaper copy." It was a

Above: Police Motorcycle Officers A.A. Winchester, left, and Leslie Ford examine the bullet-riddled money car from Agua Caliente Casino in Tijuana, looted in a daylight murder-holdup in 1929. Below: 1927 photograph of a San Diego police motorcycle squad racked up in front of the station on Second Street, between F and G streets. Riders, left to right, Earl Martin, Bert W. Johnston, Frank V. Merritt, Harry Travis, and Charles H. Graham.

By 1927, when this picture was taken, San Diego police had amassed a motley collection of motor vehicles, as this lineup in the 700 block of Second Street shows. Starting at left, the "Old Grey Goose" Cadillac ambulance, a Dodge ambulance, and then privately-owned touring cars used for suburban patrol. The city paid each officer $50 monthly for the use of a car while on duty.

clear case of interference by politicians who wanted the police to wink at certain violations of law.

A month before Hill was to finish his two-year term as chief, Walter Austin defeated the incumbent in the city election and became the new mayor. A newspaper, the *San Diego Progress*, in its election story spelled out Hill's fate: "It is not likely Chief Hill, appointed by Mayor Clark, will be reappointed."

That same election on April 7, 1931, produced a result much more momentous for the history of the Police Department than the fate of a single chief. The voters of the city approved a new charter, one calling for the city manager form of government, a charter which survives to the present day but which proved nearly unworkable at first.

"The necessity of reform in city government, so obvious for years in politics and in the administration of the Police Department, produced a new city charter," historian Richard Pourade wrote in *The Rising Tide*. "The question whether the city manager system instituted by the voters was to survive, let alone govern, remained in doubt during much of the Depression.

"Underlying the struggle was whether San Diego would be an open or closed town. City councilmen, long accustomed to personal powers and the manipulation of the Police

Department, were wary of the city manager system approved by the people."

The new charter replaced the old one, framed by freeholders and adopted in 1889, and amended so many times during the years that one news editor referred to it as a "patched pot." The 1931 charter was the result of four years of effort, dating back to the formation of a Board of Freeholders in 1928.

The new charter provided for a City Council of six members, nominated by districts and elected at large. The mayor was nominated and elected at large and was a seventh member; the mayor presided at council meetings and was delegated to do the ceremonial honors for the city.

This charter was one of many compromises. The fire and police chiefs were to be appointed by the city manager subject to approval by the council. The term of office was indefinite; no longer would the chief have to face the uncertainty of reappointment every two years. The city manager could remove a chief of either department, but all hearings involving investigation of the reasons for removal must be conducted by the council. Police and firemen were to be recruited by the city Civil Service Commission; but once they were appointed, the commission had no further control. A merit system was to be set up by each department for its own

Percy Benbough. Prosperous businessman who tried to reorganize the demoralized force but failed.

Wesley S. Sharp. Shown in his recruit uniform in 1931. He later was to head the force.

Harry H. Scott. Texan and retired Navy man. He lasted only ten months as chief.

rating and promotional procedures.

The Fire Department received two concessions: Fire chiefs were to be chosen by the city manager from the ranks, and the double platoon system was not to be altered or tampered with by the city manager. The city manager was given full administrative authority over all other departments. With police and fire department support as well as the support of the three daily newspapers—the *Union*, *Tribune*, and *Sun*—the proposal passed and became effective in 1932. The *Union* called the new charter a "clear-cut manager form of government."

It was a good charter, but at first, particularly in the first three years, the effect on the Police Department was disastrous.

Wesley Sharp, who joined the force in 1931, said that between that year and 1939 he served under ten chiefs of police, including one acting chief.

Walter W. Austin, a down-to-earth businessman, was the last mayor to be elected under the 1889 charter, taking office in 1931 and serving for only one year. It was Austin who on May 4, 1931, named Percy Benbough, a prosperous undertaker, to succeed Arthur Hill as police chief; Mayor Austin told the press Benbough's term was to be only six months. Hill continued to serve on the force for four more years before retirement.

Benbough, a native of England who with his family had come to San Diego in 1889, had been active in civic affairs since his early twenties. From 1913 to 1917 he served as city councilman and also was superintendent of the Fire Department. He knew his way around City Hall.

Within a week, with his usual enthusiasm, he moved a lot of officers around the force, among them Lieutenant George Sears, who had been the detective in charge of the powerful and independent vice squad for most of the last eleven years. Benbough proposed to replace the vice squad with a morals squad and assigned Sears to a detective division desk job. For the first time in eight years Sears was back in uniform, answering telephones on the graveyard shift. It was the beginning of a long feud between the two men. They became bitter political enemies later when Benbough was mayor and Sears chief.

Benbough made a valiant effort as chief but resigned in three months, effective August 3, 1931. In his resignation letter Benbough was blunt: "A department allowed to deteriorate for fifteen years cannot be reorganized and brought to a stage of perfection overnight."

One of the three deputy chiefs appointed by Benbough, James Patrick, was made acting chief, the third time he had taken temporary command.

On August 26, Mayor Austin sprang a surprise, naming Harry H. Scott to be chief. The council gave unanimous approval. Scott came to San Diego from Fort Worth, Texas, where he was secretary to the police chief. Before entering civil service work he had served fourteen years in the Navy, retiring in 1921 with a gunner's rating. At the time of his appointment as chief he still carried a badge from the Fort Worth police.

After Benbough quit, Mayor Austin asked the city Civil

Service Commission, as a tool of reorganization, to investigate the Police Department. The commission made its report on November 30, 1931, after looking into the "material, physical, and personnel" aspects of the department, and came to these conclusions:

"What is the matter with the Police Department? We would say that the following elements have a powerful influence to stop progress in the department. (1) The uncertainty of length of office of the chief of police. (2) The improper method of selection of a chief. Selection of a chief by political influence, rather than for character and merit. (3) Lack of support of the chief in his administration of office."

In other conclusions, numbered 4 through 15, the commission listed other negative influences: outside interference, politics within the department, lack of discipline, lack of proper schooling and training of police officers, lack of modern methods, lack of cooperation between various elements within the force, lack of confidence by men in the department, lack of a real merit system, poor physical condition of some members of the department, lack of ambition of some officers, lack of modern equipment, and lack of esprit de corps.

"Otherwise, the department is a model police department" was the tongue-in-cheek conclusion, with this footnote:

"Every one of the above-named hindrances for progress can be remedied, and with proper management and planning we believe can be done at very little expense to the taxpayers if the proper support is given the department."

Then the commission got to the bottom line:

The very nature of the duties of a police department differ from all other departments of the city, and the duties become more complex as the city progresses.

We are proud of our Fire Department, but it is unfair to the Police Department to compare it with the Fire Department. The efficient Fire Department saves our wealth, our homes, our business, prevents chaos in our business and lowers our insurance rates. It is seldom seen except in action.

A rare moment in San Diego police history was captured in this photograph, the only time Mayor Percy Benbough (left) and Police Chief George Sears, political enemies, shook hands. The occasion was the gift in mid-1930s by Benbough of the big black horse, "Dan," shown in background with Officer Frank Bonnet in the saddle. Dan was used for patrol on the 1935 Exposition grounds.

Whereas, our Police Department is looked upon as a necessary evil, is constantly between two or more fires and efficient or inefficient, it is condemned at all times by some group of our citizens.

When the police close a gambling room, a bootlegging joint or a house of prostitution, the result is not alone the enmity of those arrested, but in many cases the ill-will of the owner of the premises rented by the law violator. Also the ill-will of the merchants, the cafe owner, and others who received patronage from the offenders.

Leading citizens appeal to the mayor, the councilman, and others who are supposed to have influence with the Police Department to stop the prosecution of the arrested parties.

The hue and cry is raised that the Police Department is killing the town. The plea is made that gambling, drinking, and lust are natural pursuits of many of our otherwise law-abiding citizens and the ever-present argument, "You forget that San Diego is a seaport town and that you are always going to have gambling, drinking and ladies of easy virtue in a seaport town."

Failure to arrest the gambler, bootlegger, and others of the vice element is met by the cry from our good people: Get a new chief. The bootlegging racket is a big business, not only in San Diego but in all cities. We know it to be a flourishing business in San Diego; bootleggers cannot exist without patrons, who are also law violators. Then we have the petty law violator, the merchant who obstructs the sidewalk with his wares, the ever-present violator who insists on traveling forty-five miles an hour in a twenty-mile zone and other violators too numerous to mention, who are all inclined to cry out, Down with the chief! Get a new chief!

It is well to dwell upon another angle of the police question: The public is going to have just the police department they want, when they really make up their mind what they want.

That was a candid and most damning description of what was wrong with the Police Department between the two world

Left: During the prohibition days Mike Shea (with gun) and Richard Chadwick pose in front of a truck loaded with confiscated "alky" tins. Right: Customs Officer C.M. Whitaker and a confiscated "Booze Car."

wars. It did not lead to any immediate reform, but it showed the way. Concrete evidence was lacking to point the finger at any officers suspected of corrupt practices. Despite numerous rumors relative to collusion between the police and bookmakers, none could be verified.

Meanwhile the Texan, Scott, served less than ten months, losing his job when a new city administration took over on June 11, 1932.

At this point the Police Department came for the first time under the city manager. The department also entered the era of cliques. "The turnover in police chiefs was so rapid we all belonged to cliques to survive," A. E. Jansen said in the last interview he gave before his death. Jansen and Wesley Sharp, who later were to hold the chief's job between them for twenty years (fourteen for Jansen and six for Sharp) had just joined the force, a year apart.

Jansen said the biggest problem during this turbulent period was that three or four members of the force were trying to be the chief, and that made three or four factions. "The cliques filled up the station house and overflowed out on the sidewalk. They would be in a corner or on the street, all whispering about who was going to be this or that, cutting it all up

between them, all before their man actually was appointed chief. You were either in or out in those days. You pretty much had to know what was going on. Those that didn't know were just the 'soldiers' of the force and they weren't entitled to anything and didn't get anything."

Sergeant Earnest A. L. "Nellie" Nelson, whose colorful police career started as chauffeur of the Model T Ford lifeguard rescue truck at Ocean Beach and Mission Beach, told how it was to be an ordinary soldier:

"Back in the early Thirties things were really tough. I rode the trolley to work at the downtown station from my East San Diego home. At Thirtieth and University, a transfer stop, I would buy a morning paper from a newsboy to find out who was chief of police that day."

In April 1932 John F. Forward, Jr., was elected mayor, first to hold that office under the new city manager charter. The first city manager was appointed a month later; like his three immediate successors, however, he never had a chance. They served for months, not years. They were Horace Harvey Esselstyn (May to July 1932); A.V. Goeddel (July 1932 to May 1933); Fred W. Lockwood (May 1933 to August 1934); and George L. Buck (August 1934 to August 1935).

The first manager, Esselstyn, a public works commissioner of Detroit, Michigan, appointed an old pro, John T. Peterson, one of Benbough's deputy chiefs, as chief effective June 12, 1932. Peterson, born in 1880 in Leavenworth, Indiana, joined the force March 11, 1912; made detective June 1, 1914; and detective sergeant, June 21, 1922. At the time he took command of the force he was a detective lieutenant. Esselstyn, who said he acted quickly because suspense was hurting the force, believed that Peterson would increase efficiency and reorganize the department along the lines provided by the charter.

Peterson holds a unique niche in police history. He was the first police chief to be appointed by a city manager and was a police chief for three separate terms, first for fifty days in June and July of 1932; again for a year, from September 1932 to September 1933; and last, for eight

Top: Four of the famous "dry squad" raiders of Prohibition days with a confiscated alcohol still and other paraphernalia from an illegal plant on Cottonwood Street, ca. 1930. Left to right, Sgt. Tommy Osborne, Elmer Macy (foreground), Mike Shea clowning with hose in hat and Lt. George Sears.

months, from July 1939 to March 1940. In the first two-and-a-half years of the city manager government, the city had four city managers and Peterson was either chief or acting chief under all of them. They used him as a baseball club manager might use a utility infielder.

When Goeddel, the city's purchasing agent, was made city manager, he complained publicly he was under constant pressure from councilmen. Some wanted a new chief who would stamp out sin completely; others wanted the cops to go easy in enforcing the law, particularly against their cronies.

In this atmosphere it is not surprising that Goeddel picked a top policeman who knew and admired Goeddel—Captain Robert P. Newsom. Newsom's son, Robert, who retired as an inspector of the San Diego Sheriff's Office, said in a 1978 interview, "My old man was what they used to call the 'strong, silent type.' He liked Goeddel. But he hated politics, like a lot of old-time policemen."

The son also said the Masonic Order was "strong in politics all during my dad's police career, and was the dominant power in selection of a police chief. Dad was high in the order and an active Mason."

The fourth chief in little more than a year, Newsom held office only fourteen months. His term as chief was marked by

installation of one-way radios in police cars and by a new merit system for promotion.

The police radio system took years to achieve. Groundwork started under Chief Doran about 1928 and extended until December 1, 1932, when the police radio station went into operation with radio operator Vern Thompson in Balboa Park in the radio shack ordering, "All police cars stand by." It operated from 2 p.m. to 6 a.m. No code was used at first. A detective car for downtown had one radio receiver and others were installed in patrol cars in Ocean Beach, Mission Beach, La Jolla, and East San Diego.

Chief Newsom said a few words to his men over the new station, KGPZ, and later in a news interview said one radio patrol car now could cover three times the territory a patrolman did fifteen years before, and much more effectively.

"When I joined the force in 1916 we had five horses, the auto used by Chief Keno Wilson, and three motorcycles. I could walk my Logan Heights beat only twice during a shift. Now one radio patrol car covers a much larger territory, and more thoroughly. In my opinion, a patrolman in a radio car can do more work more efficiently in an eight-hour period than a foot patrolman could do in a month."

Until patrol cars were equipped with transmitters for

John T. Peterson. "Pete" was popular with the rank and file in the 1930s and served three separate terms as chief.

Robert P. Newsom, an army veteran, was known as a "strong silent type" chief who hated politics.

Harry J. Raymond. Imported from Los Angeles, he became an embarrassment as police chief and was fired.

two-way communication in 1936, the police dispatcher never knew whether the calls were received or orders had been carried out until field officers reported back, sometimes an hour later, by telephone.

As the Depression deepened, the city retrenched to meet budgetary demands. When Wesley Sharp joined the force in May 1931, he was mighty glad to be making $155 a month. "Just a month later I heard on the commercial radio that forty-one officers would have to be cut. I figured since I was one of the last appointed I would be one of those laid off. But the guys on the force chose by vote to take a cut in pay to keep everyone on the payroll."

Before August 1932, patrolmen were paid $155 to $185 monthly. Then the pay range was cut to $134.33 to $160, and by 1934 it was $120 to $150. It remained low until late in the Thirties, when the city began to recover financially.

The only serious riot since the IWW troubles in 1912 occurred on Memorial Day in 1933, during Chief Newsom's tenure. The Young Communist League of Los Angeles, barred from demonstrating there, came to San Diego. The hard times had brought a resurgence of radicalism in the country like that of 1912. The City Council denied the Young Communist League a parade permit because the group refused to promise that the Red Flag would not be displayed. An estimated three hundred members of the league were trucked to San Diego and unloaded in New Town Park, downtown. Placards against "Imperialistic War" were displayed and speakers denounced President Franklin D. Roosevelt and charged that air games over San Diego were moving the nation toward war.

Captain Yancey Adams was in charge of a special police force assigned to prevent a parade. When the league attempted to form up to parade, police charged into the ranks to grab banners and break up the demonstration. In the riot that followed, Patrolman Ray Holcomb was seriously beaten and Officer A. E. Jansen and several others were less seriously injured. (It was Jansen's only injury in his long police career.) Thirty demonstrators were hurt and several arrested. The wild melee, in which a Marine and several civilians went to the aid of police, ended with the firing of a tear-gas shell.

Chief Newsom's friend and boss, City Manager Goeddel, was forced to resign after the May 1933 elections. He quit on June 1. Newsom went home one night and told his wife he had had enough of politicians and was going to resign as chief, and he did. He reverted to his old rating of captain on June 4, 1933.

The next city manager, Fred W. Lockwood, immediately appointed an outsider, Harry J. Raymond, a private detective once employed in the Los Angeles County district attorney's office, as the new chief. The rank and file of police needed a boost in morale and a change to reform their tattered ranks, but an outsider was not the answer. The response was instant, with openly voiced suspicions that Raymond had questionable associations in Los Angeles. Lockwood replied to criticism by claiming there were three or four cliques in the department and only an outside man could break them up.

To sum up Raymond's brief administration (June 5 to September 3, 1933) the late Police Inspector Louis C. Schnug said, "Things kinda got away from him."

This is one of the patrol watches posed on the sidewalk outside of the police station at 732 Second Street in June, 1931. In the front row, left to right, first uniformed officer, Sgt. M. R. Zimmerman, Lt. Glenn Treleaven, Walter Macy, superintendent of identification bureau; and Police Chief Robert Newsom. The woman on the left is Mrs. M. B. Veall, a matron. The woman on the right is Marie Remington, a telephone operator. In the second row, far right, is Patrolman Jasper Davis.

It was a kindly summary. After weathering cries of underworld connections, Raymond juggled details around and shifted ranking officers to outlying stations. Police raids and surveillance pressure on cafes selling beer aroused the ire of businessmen. On September 2, rumors that Raymond had resigned and left the city flew about. The next morning the *Union* bannered the front page "Raymond Fired," with a story in which City Manager Lockwood said: "Raymond is not the man for the job. He can't reorganize the department. He has shown no executive ability. He is temperamentally unfit for the post. I think these are reasons enough."

Lieutenant John T. Peterson, who had been sent out to pasture at the East San Diego substation, was appointed police chief for the second time, this time for a full year, not just for a few weeks. But again it was just a caretaker term. Chief "Pete" recalled the faithful from outlying posts where Raymond had shunted them and again strengthened the detective division.

Early in 1934 Mayor Forward, in poor health and upset by politics, resigned, as did two councilmen. The council appointed Rutherford B. Irones, a physician, to fill the unexpired term of mayor. Then Lockwood resigned, and in came a new city manager, George L. Buck. Two days later, it was Chief Peterson's turn to resign (effective September 6, 1934), and he retired soon after.

Detective Lieutenant George Sears, the head of the vice squad and mostly associated with enforcement of dry laws, was chosen by Buck as police chief. With this appointment, the door to the chief's office stopped revolving.

Chapter 13
THE SEARS YEARS

If there was to be stability in administration of the Police Department, George Sears, a veteran who knew his job, had to be a strong man. And he was. He fought a mayor who was his political arch-enemy for years, and fought him to a stand-still, but finally Chief Sears gave up the battle.

He was something of an enigma—to his friends a shrewd and seasoned political tactician, to his critics a corrupt cop on whom they could never get the goods.

"Sears was active, determined, strong; the most aggressive officer I ever knew," Wesley Sharp said in tribute to one of the ten chiefs he served under during his first ten years on the force. "Sears came from Colorado and was nicknamed 'The Cowboy.' He could be a real rough guy when it was necessary. Nobody scared him. He and Dick Chadwick were detectives who had reputations in the early Thirties. The town was quiet except for the raids on bootleggers and stills, and other crack-downs by the vice squad. Sears and Chadwick were a team and drew most of the widely publicized assignments. They did a good job. Because the vice squad work made the bulk of police news, about everyone in town knew Sears and Chadwick were police detectives, even if they didn't know anyone else on the force."

An officer who worked with "The Cowboy" many years, Inspector Louis Schnug, said of Sears: "He was a real police-man, possibly the first chief to start reorganizing the depart-ment to put it on a higher plane. He was a man of strong prin-ciples who wanted everyone under him to be the same way.

"By the time he became chief, Sears was worth at least a half million dollars. The Sears family was the Cuyamaca Meat Company and the Cuyamaca Bank in El Cajon, and owned a lot of property in the El Cajon Valley. George had a nice home in Point Loma.

"There was no reason in the world for him to become involved in anything petty and he ran an honest department."

When George Sears became the twenty-second police chief, he had been a resident of the county continuously since 1906. Born in 1885 at Rye, Colorado, he got his education in Pueblo. George acquired wide knowledge of San Diego city and county affairs over the years. He was associated with his father for many years in cattle raising and general ranching in Julian, El Cajon, and the Jamul areas. He served as a county fire warden, assigned to the Cleveland National Forest; served four years as deputy county assessor; and was with the D. C. Collier Realty Company, specializing in ranch properties.

Sears was appointed a patrolman on January 27, 1915, by Chief Keno Wilson, and advanced through the ranks to detec-tive lieutenant. He married Lucille Griffin, daughter of Ida Griffin, the first full-time police matron. Ida Griffin was a widow when she joined the Police Department and she later married Police Captain Arthur R. Hill, who became chief in 1929.

After Sears was named police chief, he transferred a num-ber of ranking officers, and then picked Captain Hill (who had reverted to that rank after stepping down as chief) as assistant chief, a position that had been vacant two years. This brought immediate criticism of nepotism from the crusading *Sun*, which said, "It will be difficult to forget that Captain Hill is related by marriage to the chief."

What kept Sears in office for four years and seven months was the support he received from city managers George Buck and R. W. Flack. Flack succeeded Buck after the spring elec-tion of 1935, which swept into office the former short-time police chief, Percy Benbough, as mayor, along with six coun-cilmen who were loyal to the new charter and were pledged to good government under it.

Percival James Benbough and George Meredith Sears had been antagonists four years earlier when Benbough was chief, and the antagonism sharpened when Benbough became mayor. Benbough came into sharp conflict with the council-men over administration of the Police Department. Wanting to deal directly with police and not through the manager's office, he chafed under the restraints the charter imposed on the power of the mayor. But his attitude was a throwback to the bad old days and Sears wasn't about to turn over any of his authority over the department, especially not to Benbough. Eventually Benbough went public and tried to get the man-ager to fire Sears. Failing in this attempt, Benbough tried to line up an alliance of policemen to attack the police merit sys-tem and accused police of accepting graft from vice interests. Eventually, Benbough wanted both Sears and Flack fired, but against this demand the council held firm.

An eight-page tabloid newspaper entitled "Election Campaign Souvenir," which was published in 1939 by the League for Civic Action, had this comment to make on city politics:

"Chief Sears is the riddle of local politics. Going on five years now, there never had been a day when Percy Benbough wouldn't have laid $1,000 on the line for evidence that would really hook Sears on a graft charge. Every stool pigeon in town, every cop-hater, every grifter had known this. Nobody has produced the evidence yet. The wise guys will never suspect that the chief might be just an ordinary guy, doing the day's work."

A clue to Sears's staying power is given by Richard Pourade, who was a top crime reporter for the *Sun* during this period. In his *Rising Tide*, Pourade wrote that "no suspicion of wrongdoing attached to council members elected by the Civic Affairs Conference, but they supported the manager and chief of police in a policy of an 'open town' because of San Diego's status as a tourist city and a military center."

In any event, prostitution and gambling flourished. The problem of bootlegging had vanished with the end of Prohibition in December 1933. But as long as prostitution and gambling were

Police Chief Sears. He lost the battle, won the war for the department.

winked at, there was the possibility of official corruption.

Elmer Jansen in 1978 said of Sears, "The only trouble with Sears was being a politician—a real good one."

Robert Karrow, a retired police lieutenant who was appointed to the force by Sears and who for many months worked directly under the chief as an undercover officer, had this to say:

> Were Chief Sears and the politicians wrong in allowing houses of prostitution? From my experience I would say no. Compared with today [1980], prostitution then was under control. The prostitutes were part of the control. They simply did not want street competition and would inform the police about such competition.

> Although some houses of prostitution were known to exist, there was no license for streetwalkers, bar prostitutes, or women working the "profession," out of hotels as individuals. I don't think any police department can completely obliterate prostitution. If you close the houses they spread out into the city, become massage parlors, and so on.

But official toleration for vice diminished as the city proudly prepared for the opening of another big Exposition in Balboa Park. City leaders in 1935, like those in 1915, wanted to give Exposition visitors to San Diego an impression of civic purity. At these times they brushed aside the argument that the city had to be open to harmless vice in order to attract business.

So it could have been predicted that what was left of the Stingaree would become a target. Headlines in the three daily newspapers on February 14, 1935, reported unusual raids made by the county district attorney, Thomas Whelan, and police.

The *Union*—"Drive Made by Whelan and Police, Double-Barreled Clean-up Fills City, County Jails; D. A. Men Hack Down Door in Spectacular Sweep." Next day, "Stirred by Arrest In Chinatown, City Hall Agog after Tom Quin is Caught in Raid by Whelan's Men; Police are Taken by Surprise."

The *Sun*—"Tom Quin, 86 Others Jailed in Whelan Raid; Lotteries 'Cleanup' Target."

The *Tribune*—"Doors Shut by Courts, Is Sears Proposal."

The newspapers had a field day in their coverage of the sudden raids by the D. A., who sent two squads of special investigators to do the work while he dined with City Manager George Buck and a councilman at the Emerald Hills Country Club. The Chinatown raids started at 9:30 p.m. and netted thirty-six Chinese men, including Tom Ah Quin, described by the *Sun* as "overlord" and "mayor of Chinatown" and as "conferee of public officials, influencer of City Hall appointments, and generally recognized boss of certain political elements." The *Sun* added that Quin's arrest (the first for him) "caused the most blink-eyed amazement."

Police weren't exactly caught napping by the D. A. and his special squads. Within an hour, the police responded with their own raids. Sears sent his vice squad officers, led by Sergeant E. Tom Osborne, into Chinatown to make fifty-one arrests, topping the D. A.'s arrest total.

In the second-day coverage of the raids, the *Union* had this comment: "Quin's Fifth Avenue restaurant has been a meeting place in the past for a number of councilmen, who usually explain their visits on the ground that Quin had an excellent cook who knew how Chinese dishes should be

Opening day, May 29, 1935, at the California Pacific International Exposition. A special police detail led by Chief George M. Sears (front of lead sedan saluting) welcomes dignitaries in a guarded car.

D. A. Whelan was next to inform the public that only his agents knew of the impending raids, adding they were an effort to "assist the chief of police because of any political pressure which might have been brought to bear on him."

The incident faded away, the accused gamblers lost an appeal, and Quin (a native of San Diego) and others arrested paid a total of $1,725 in fines.

Despite all the gambling raid confusion, the year 1935 was a vintage year for Sears and his administration. He had warned his officers to save money toward purchase of new blue uniforms to be worn by opening day of the California Pacific International Exposition in Balboa Park on May 29. This second fair was to run through 1935 and on until November 11, 1936. The uniform adopted was blue with Sam Browne belt. The original blue uniform was worn from 1889 through World War I. In 1919–1920, the uniform was changed to an olive-drab, khaki doughboy style, with choker collar. History was to repeat itself in 1947, when the department gradually began to change back from blue to the present tan uniform.

In this second Exposition police had complete charge of security, and a score of selected officers were assigned to park duty, including two mounted on horses. Sears eventually had four mounted officers. The most challenging jobs for the fair detail—and the ones that worried Sears the most—were keeping the girly exhibit under control and preventing illegal gambling in the "Gold Gulch" replica of an old mining town in a park canyon.

prepared. Several of the meetings attracted citywide attention as they came on the eve of important changes in municipal officeholders, and one was the subject of a grand jury quiz."

Throughout the news blitz, City Manager Buck backed Chief Sears and said he welcomed the cooperation of the district attorney as the Police Department was "greatly undermanned."

By the time Sears finished his first year as chief, Buck was out as manager and Dr. Rutherford Irones, who had been appointed mayor to finish Forward's unexpired term, was in jail. The council had paid $2,700 for a limousine (dubbed "the

Above: Old Gamewell Call System, downtown San Diego, ca. 1913.
Right: Frank Bonnet, Mounted Patrol, 1935 Exposition.

Royal Coach" by the press) for the mayor's official use. Irones was driving this car when involved in a collision with an auto driven by a sailor, whose wife was injured. Irones had been drinking and failed to stop. While rumors were floating all over town, police did nothing. A newspaper investigation and a civil suit for personal injury damages led to belated filing of hit-run charges against the mayor. Irones resigned the office just before he was convicted and sentenced to six months in jail.

By that time, Sears's nemesis, Benbough, had been elected mayor in the spring 1935 elections.

Patrolman Walter O'Haver made trouble for Sears for more than a year by charging vice and graft existed throughout city and county government. The officer appeared before the City Council in 1938 and demanded a public hearing. O'Haver forced a grand jury investigation. The grand jury and city attorney announced that graft and payoff charges had been thoroughly investigated and none of O'Haver's accusations could be substantiated "in a single instance."

O'Haver was dismissed from the force but won reinstatement and retired from the department on pension in 1949 with twenty years of service.

Despite the constant infighting with Benbough and the recurring suspicions of police corruption, Sears provided the Police Department with desperately needed stability after rough times and resisted all efforts to discredit or remove him in his more than four years as chief, proving that he should be considered one of the superchiefs. Among his accomplishments were the modernization of the radio communication system, the organization of the Junior Traffic Patrol by the Police Department, and construction of a new jail and police station.

Veterans recalling the old one-way radio system likened it to "flying on one wing." Calls were beamed to five Model A Ford patrol cars. Field officers had to find a telephone or call box to report back. W. D. Thompson, an inventor, was the designer and consultant in developing the two-way system. A transmitter was installed under the dashboard in cars, a control switch on the steering wheel, and speakers overhead. The remotely controlled central transmitter was called Radio KGPZ. Two-way communication started in April 1935 and was improved when broadcasting equipment was moved in 1939 to the earthquake-proof city fire-alarm building in Balboa Park.

Into the 1950s, Radio KGPZ served not only the San Diego cops but also the Sheriff's Office; the police of

Above: A long overdue new police headquarters, jail and courtrooms becomes a reality. On August 2, 1938 this groundbreaking ceremony was held on tidelands at 801 West Market Street, attended by San Diego city council members, City Manager Robert W. Flack, and Chief Sears, who are on the platform below the steam boiler. Mayor Percy Benbough refused the invitation to participate. He had opposed the building.

Left: Police vehicles of all types, an ambulance at the gasoline pumps, motorcycles, marked and unmarked cars are parked in the spacious garage at the new Market Street headquarters. Chief Sears predicted this area would not be crowded for fifty years. Within ten years the department was scrambling for more space.

Coronado, National City, Chula Vista and El Cajon; and the California Highway Patrol. The Gamewell network of call boxes with red call lights at intersections, installed under Chief Keno Wilson in 1913, was retained.

Sears took an active part in creation of the Junior Traffic Patrol. In the early 1930s the school system expanded and motor vehicle traffic accidents near schools were causing about twenty-five student injury cases a year. Federal Works Progress Administration crossing guards were tried at some schools. City Manager Flack authorized Sears to take Sergeant

Frank Merritt with him on a tour of other cities to inspect school patrols. The results of this study produced the patrol system used since 1935, in which selected fourth-, fifth-, and sixth-graders are trained to stop auto traffic safely while children cross the street.

On the fiftieth anniversary of the patrol in 1985, it was reported that only half a dozen minor accidents had occurred at patrolled crossings in the half-century. At that time, Sergeant Dorothy Hutchinson was directing a program that enlisted some two thousand young guards in most of the city's

107

elementary schools. The corps included girls, admitted for the first time in 1972, the same year the Police Department opened field duty to women.

In the summer of 1935 one of the problems facing City Manager Flack was the need for a new jail and police headquarters. In the period 1925–1927, Jerry MacMullen, the late historian, was a young police reporter on the *Tribune*. He recalled, "When they said we had a lousy jail they weren't kidding. Many times after being in that old jail on Second Street I went home and washed lice out of my hair."

The city was trying to follow the Nolen Plan, a master plan for urban development drafted early in the century. It called for the creation of a mall with the Civic Center as the anchor and government buildings continuing up Cedar Street to Balboa Park.

School patrol mascot, ca. 1938.

police headquarters building and jail unlike any police headquarters in the United States. It combined exterior beauty with interior efficiency.

Architects created a "Hall of Justice" wing on the southwest corner of the site, across from the Coronado ferry slip, to house five municipal courts soon to be created from the old justice of the peace courts. Only one of these, Department 5, Judge John J. Brennan presiding, was ever occupied. Brennan's "Police Court" was connected to the City Jail by a closed corridor. The remaining four courtrooms eventually were converted to police use.

The new jail was a fortress made of heavier-grade concrete. Its capacity when opened was 188 prisoners, which increased to 288 by the time it was closed in 1974. Of six cell blocks, one was exclusively for women.

The cost rose to $390,000

At first the police station (to include a city jail) was suggested for the mall. This caused a flurry of protests—no one wanted a jail on the mall.

Nearly three years passed before a location on public tidelands, on Market Street between Kettner Boulevard and Pacific Highway, was approved. This was an area earmarked for development as a park. The Harbor Commission gave occupancy to the city for as long as the tidelands would be used by a police facility.

Coronado residents objected, fearing that the new jail would be offensive to their eyes and ears as they went to and from the nearby ferry slip. So the architects made the rear of the jail on what later was Harbor Drive look as much unlike a jail as possible, with a high wall to shield it from view.

"PWA Aid Sought," the *Union* headline announced November 21, 1936, in reporting on preliminary plans for a new police headquarters, courtrooms, and jail. The federal Public Works Administration was asked for a grant of $145,000 to aid in the construction.

What was built was a long, low, rambling structure around a huge inner courtyard with waving palm trees against the background of red tile, accenting the Spanish design. Rising on four square blocks of reclaimed tidelands was a

with the federal grant paying $166,500. Other costs ran the total to a little over $400,000.

Chief Sears was in the forefront of the proponents of the building project, and Mayor Benbough was the lone dissenter on the council. The mayor fought a losing battle.

Almost every morning during the construction, Chief Sears would have an aide drive him down to the site. "He didn't know much about construction, but he liked to watch the progress of the building," Wesley Sharp said. "Mayor Benbough had his way only once with Sears over the police building—Sears was forced into retirement before it was finished and he never occupied it." By the time the order came for the move-in (May 8, 1939), Sears was a private citizen, swept into retirement by Benbough's sweeping re-election victory at the polls. The election was held April 25, 1939, and Sears quit two days later.

The spring elections of 1939 had given Mayor Benbough the opportunity to win what he had been seeking for two years—more political clout. He announced for re-election and put up two council candidates. He promised to "mow them down" and he did. Benbough in his victory speech said Manager Flack and Chief Sears were to go, and they did. Benbough had been overwhelmingly supported by the people,

These three pictures were taken in 1939 about the time workmen were finishing up the new headquarters at 801 West Market Street. Top left: the stately tower which housed the police radio in the first years. Top right: the patio with the view looking northeast and the palm tree in the traffic circle. Below: an excellent aerial view showing the general area. The two buildings in front of headquarters (left at Kettner Boulevard and Market Street) were removed before the station was occupied. The Coronado ferry is upper right.

Left: Tile for the roof of the new police headquarters at the foot of Market Street is stacked in a storage lot on the bayside of the construction site. Right: This is an aerial photograph of the headquarters as it appeared late in the 1960s after extensive remodeling, which added air conditioning and other improvements. Vacant bayside land at top is now occupied by Seaport Village.

and Flack and Sears saw the writing on the wall—their time was over. When he resigned in May 1939, Flack had served more than four years, a record for a city manager at that time. Sears served four years and seven months, not a record but a respectable performance and a great contrast to the brief terms of his immediate predecessors in the chief's office.

Pourade summarized the Sears years: "The people wanted a different kind of a city, the concept of an 'open town' was gradually abandoned and the Police Department was reorganized along more professional lines.

"[Benbough] had surmounted all his enemies and driven those who opposed him from power. He had cleaned up the town and broken an alliance between the 'blue-stocking' City Council and a city administration and Police Department which had contended that gambling and prostitution were natural and desirable in a city dependent so heavily on tourists and on a Navy enlisted personnel which at that time was composed largely of unmarried men."

When Sears threw in the towel, the *Union* said he "beat his political opponents to the draw." When he retired, Sears turned his back on twenty-four years of police work, receiving half of his $375-a-month chief's salary. His retirement was quickly approved and became effective immediately. In a letter to City Manager Flack, Sears said he was retiring "in view of the present political situation and in the interests of harmony in the forthcoming reorganization of the city administration."

In his retirement, Sears made an unsuccessful bid for the post of county supervisor from the First District in 1944. Service as an appointed police chief does not often translate into voter support for elective office.

George Sears was the last in a long line of San Diego police chiefs to fall victim to city politics in the Thirties. But his strong independence in the chief's office paid off for later chiefs. Beginning in 1939, as the Police Department achieved more autonomy, the chiefs began to outlast changes in the city manager's office and the mayor's office. One factor was the ability of the new professional chiefs to gain public support in their own right. Another factor was the growing public support for city managers. That made it politically impossible for new mayors to fire a manager or for new managers to fire a police chief simply in order to put their own men in office.

George Sears lost his battle with Benbough, but he won the war for the department.

Chapter 14
PETERSON THE PROFESSIONAL

The loose partnership which had long fostered gambling and prostitution in San Diego "because they're good for a tourist and Navy town" was fast coming unglued. World War II was just around the corner and it would bring vast changes in San Diego, paving the way for a modern police department. The days of the quiet town were over.

The second great war put an end to the political squabbling which had disorganized and demoralized the Police Department for years. Organized prostitution was wiped out at the behest of the Navy. When the word came down to the city fathers in 1942 that the Western Defense Command wanted the bawdy houses closed, they were closed. The rationale for continuing to countenance them disappeared overnight and never was heard again. The women spread out over the city and continued in business, as Keno Wilson had predicted, but they were on their own. No longer did they have powerful protectors in the person of landlords with political influence. No longer was there so strong an incentive for law enforcers to look the other way. When San Diego ceased to be an open town, Tijuana, across the nearby border in Mexico, took its place as a pleasure spot for lonely servicemen. The economy of San Diego had more important and more lucrative things to do. The era of corruption in city government was nearing the end.

When George Sears "pulled the pin" and went into retirement in the spring of 1939, Chief of Detectives Harry J. Kelly, a veteran of twenty-two years, took over the force temporarily. The press pointed out that chief after chief for years had stepped into the top job, only to realize in a few months, a few weeks, or even a few hours his inability to cope with interference from politicians and the discord within the department.

Kelly served as acting chief nearly four months, playing it safe, chasing hawkers for card games and bookies off the streets, and restricting himself to a caretaker's role. While he held the fort, there was much speculation over who would become the next chief. One reporter said the names mentioned "sounded like a roll call of the department."

On July 18, 1939, City Manager Fred A. Rhodes notified the City Council he had asked John T. Peterson, twice former chief, to come out of retirement and for the third time take over the top spot. The council confirmed the appointment. Peterson said, "I'll have to get acquainted again with the force." Kelly went back to captain of detectives, heading a division consisting of twenty-three detectives. Peterson said

there would be no purge nor forced retirement but added, "Some with twenty years should retire." He said he had no axe to grind and promised a square deal.

San Diego was beginning to feel the influx of service personnel and civilian defense workers. Construction of Navy facilities bolstered the city's economy. After the move to new headquarters, every phase of police work expanded. J. T. Peterson's third and last term as chief lasted eight months and six days. Then on March 20, 1940, he went back into retirement when the city manager asked him to resign. The search for a police chief was over and the choice was to the liking of Mayor Benbough. It was a man from out of town, willing to conduct a purge if necessary to reorganize the force, and one without friends among ranking officers.

The outsider was Clifford E. Peterson, thirty-nine, a lieutenant of the Long Beach Police Department with seventeen years of service. He had experience in police training and traffic administration and was a graduate of the Federal Bureau of Investigation's National Police Academy in Washington, D. C., chosen there as president of his academy class.

When he took command of the force on March 21, 1940, San Diego was emerging from its provincial past and was soon to become a booming city of national importance. The population was 203,341 and by 1944 had swelled to 286,000. The war caused emergency expansion of all military bases in the city and county. The Navy opened Camp Elliott on Kearny Mesa and the Amphibious Base on the Silver Strand and took over part of Balboa Park. The Army built Camp Callan on Torrey Pines Mesa.

As the war intensified in the Pacific, San Diego became a major staging base. From 1940 to 1944 the 25,000 defense workers nearly quadrupled. B-24 bombers and PBY seaplanes rolled out of Consolidated-Vultee Aircraft by the thousands. Linda Vista, a federal housing project, blossomed on Kearny Mesa, becoming home for 14,000 newcomers.

A. E. Jansen, later to be chief, was then a patrol captain. He recalled that at the start of the war there were eight patrol cars—three downtown, two each in Ocean Beach and East San Diego, and one in La Jolla. The areas around downtown San Diego and Logan Heights were heavily populated. Encanto was barely settled. Clairemont and Linda Vista did not exist. There was hardly any settlement north of Mission Valley from Morena Boulevard east.

Sailors ("White Hats" to the cops) and civilian war plant workers crowded the downtown area day and night. "As patrol captain, part of my job was to make an inspection downtown on the day shift," Jansen recalled. "You could get into a fight real quick. Thousands were downtown at all hours. The police had no trouble in La Jolla from the soldiers. All the problems were downtown and at Ocean Beach."

The war changed hours for police officers, who went from a five-day work week with consecutive days off to twelve hours on, twelve hours off, seven days a week. Luckily, oral and written examinations for appointment to the force had been given in April 1939, and 81 out of 208 applicants were certified to a two-year eligibility list. On August 1, 1941, before the war drained away many officers, the Police Department reached a strength of 301 employees. That brought the ratio up to one policeman for each 1,000 residents.

Peterson began making changes.

Clifford E. Peterson. He served as police chief during hectic World War II period.

A juvenile division, the first independent juvenile division for the department, was established. Before, the juvenile bureau was part of the detective division. Now it would have its own commanding officer, who would report directly to the chief. Peterson cited this as a crime prevention function and said the duties of juvenile officers would be twofold: first, to prevent crime; and, second, to handle juveniles involved in violations without having to take them to court, where they would be given a criminal record.

Operation of the police property room was tightened. Complete records were ordered, so the property clerk could keep an inventory of every piece of property owned or held by the department.

A public relations detail supervised a juvenile amateur program on radio station KFSD. A baseball team was organized, outfitted by contributions from policemen, and entered in the American Legion junior baseball league with juvenile bureau officers managing and coaching. A department golf team was fielded. Arrangements were made for a summer international police pistol match at the police range.

Relations were improved between the police and other law enforcement agencies and business and civic groups. Morale in the department improved and officers were urged

to contact the chief on any matter, business or personal. A department publication, titled *Flash*, was issued weekly. Peterson believed it would help knit department morale.

"Because of the national situation which exists, surveys are being conducted by this office in cooperation with naval and military intelligence and the FBI to determine what problems might arise in an emergency," Peterson announced. A detective lieutenant acceptable to these federal agencies was assigned to work with them on subversive activities.

At the end of Peterson's first year as chief, the city manager's office urged increasing police strength, because of the rapid population increase and the expansion of the defense industry and other industries. Peterson said this would cost an additional $257,000 annually.

San Diego asked for millions in federal funds to meet defense-created problems. Crowding of downtown and the beaches by servicemen was cited. Peterson wanted sixty-six more patrolmen, eleven detectives, seven clerks and typists, eighteen motorcycle officers, four permanent and eighteen seasonal lifeguards, and more auto mechanics and telephone operators. Also needed would be lifeboats, autos, two more ambulances, and firearms. When this request was made late in 1941, the department had dwindled to 257 employees as the military services siphoned off men.

Retired Motorcycle Sergeant David Allsbrook recalled the intensive period after Peterson became chief: "They were interesting times, trying times, but we all learned much from each experience. Our training programs were modified to include possible enemy actions. But we were really not prepared for Pearl Harbor."

December 7, 1941, was a typical sunny day in San Diego. Captain Thad Seibert, the new assistant chief and personnel officer, was sitting down to Sunday dinner with his family when Chief Peterson telephoned, just after the radio news of the Japanese attack on Pearl Harbor. The chief said he thought they ought to get down to the station. "No one knew what to do, exactly," Seibert recalled, "other than to protect police headquarters and give the military what aid we could. Everyone went on twelve-hour shifts. Peterson took the night command and I was in charge of the day shift. The Navy was in short supply in the harbor and Fort Rosecrans could muster only a few Army people, so they were not much help to police."

Lieutenant Edward A. Dieckmann, serving as a policeman after twenty-one years in the Navy, was the officer acceptable to military intelligence agencies to command the newly formed police subversive detail. He was at his desk in the detective bureau when news of the Pearl Harbor attack was flashed on the radio.

"Within a few minutes all officers attached to the internal security detail were on the job, taking over the tasks for which they had been trained," Dieckmann said in 1942. "All through the day hundreds of civilians called to volunteer their services and jobs were found for most of them."

An embryo air raid system was set up and crude facilities were manned. Police just did what seemed to be needed, Seibert said. A watch was set up in the tower over the police station, manned by an officer armed with a Spanish-American War rifle, with instructions to sound an alarm if enemy planes were sighted.

With the hindsight of half a century, it seems ludicrous. But at the time it was believed anything could happen, and Pearl Harbor had proved it. The thirty Krag-Jorgensen rifles from the Spanish-American War period, called Springfield Model 98s, which police had in their armory, provided perhaps the most firepower any group in San Diego had on the night of December 7.

Seibert said that before Pearl Harbor Day police were giving confiscated BB guns from the property room to the Army at Camp Callan as substitutes for the wooden guns they had been using. The Navy sent the fleet out to sea immediately after the Pearl Harbor attack. The immediate fear was sabotage since San Diego was a major base of the Navy on the West Coast.

Dieckmann and his detail of officers spent the afternoon of December 7 setting in motion the plans. The Federal

Officer W.F. "Blackie" Blacker on beat he had many years, directing traffic on Fifth and Broadway, ca. 1943.

Bureau of Investigation's San Diego office had a list of Japanese and Japanese-American residents who were supposed to be potential enemy agents. That night G-men and cops, using about fifteen police cars, rounded up and brought in fourteen of them under arrest; the haul included radio equipment. None was ever convicted and not a single instance of espionage or sabotage was ever charged against any U. S. citizen or legal alien resident of Japanese ancestry on the Pacific Coast during the entire war. But the officers didn't know on December 7 that their zeal was unnecessary.

The first of hundreds of calls started coming in about "enemy" planes, bombs, flares, and generally suspicious occurrences. All had to be checked out. That first night the old rifles were issued to motorcycle officers and some patrol cars, and officers were sent out to patrol the La Jolla beaches, it being rumored the Japanese were to invade at that point. Officers were not given time for reliefs, and there was no radio communication with the units. A feeble and largely ineffective blackout was attempted throughout the city. Many policemen were on duty longer than twelve hours.

Carroll West was a mechanic in the police garage. He had worked at Consolidated Aircraft Company. He said he used his knowledge of a production line to start equipping all police cars for blackout. "We had just a tail light in front with a slit for the light to show and had to improvise as we went along," West said. "One night an officer drove into the police garage totally without lights and to show his plight lighted a book of matches for illumination."

Police Lieutenant Louis C. Schnug was appointed chief air raid warden and took over plans made by Dieckmann's officers. Eventually the city had 12,000 volunteer defense and fire wardens in thirty districts. A couple of months later the air raid warden organization was moved from police headquarters to the Civic Center. By that time the auxiliary police, the nucleus of the modern reserve police, had been organized.

On December 20, Dieckmann was made war duty officer in charge of a new command center in an unoccupied courtroom in the Hall of Justice area of police headquarters. Outside windows were sandbagged. A telephone network was

Officer Russell Giles stands beside his patrol car in April of 1947 while on duty in East San Diego. A Ford sedan similar to this cruiser was the mainstay of police patrol during World War II, when replacements were scarce.

installed connecting city officials to all operation centers—fire, sanitation, and others. In case of an enemy alert, the city manager and all his key department heads were to report there. From this center, internal security could use telephone or radio to contact Navy damage control for equipment needed in emergencies. Among the duties of the center was registering carrier pigeon owners and lofts, and censoring photos taken in prohibited areas.

Allsbrook recalled the start of the war:

The problem of traffic control under wartime conditions defied imagination—blackouts, detours around military and defense installations, military movements. During the first six months of war the military, fearing sabotage, would not ferry supplies across the bay; all shipments were around the Silver Strand to North Island.

Meanwhile, we had to maintain control and supervision of civilian traffic. Temporary officers were hired, and they were rushed into service without proper training. Many retired police officers, even some on disability pensions, were recalled to duty. We even had one motorcycle officer who was an Army deserter, but this was not discovered until two years after the end of the war.

Every morning and evening, traffic would back up from the Coronado ferry landing at the foot of Pacific Highway as far as First Avenue on Market Street. It was worst when the bay was fogged in. Countless hours were spent on military blockades,

detours and escorts of ammunition trucks. Fire and explosion of one ammunition truck blew up old Highway 101 in Rose Canyon and closed this main highway for four days, requiring rerouting of all traffic through La Jolla. A federal housing area was damaged.

Traffic Captain Frank Merritt (who had set up the school safety patrols for Sears) tried an experiment during the war, assigning three motorcycle officers on a special 7 p.m. to 3 a.m. shift, which worked until 4 a.m. on weekends. This put motorcycle officers on street patrol after midnight for the first time. Cruising the main traffic arteries, they wrote tickets like crazy which caused a public uproar.

Retired Lieutenant James Harrell, hired as a rookie shortly before Pearl Harbor, recalled this conversation with the patrol captain when he reported for duty without any training: "Captain, what am I supposed to do?" The captain: "Do you know right from wrong? If you see someone doing something wrong and there is a violation of the law, bring them down and we'll put them in jail."

"Downtown it was wall-to-wall with White Hats—English, French, American, you name it," Harrell said. "Most of the time we walked the downtown beats, but later had two-man cars. If there was trouble and you had to break it up, you did it lightning fast or the buddies of the 'White Hat' you wanted would overpower the police unit. The trick we learned was to grab the suspect and toss him into a cruiser while your partner waited behind the wheel, the engine running. Then you spun your wheels and got out of there. We would drive out of the trouble area, find a call box and summon the paddy wagon to take the prisoner to jail."

Bruce Weston, the chief jailer, prepared a procedure in case of enemy attack. A jailer would be assigned to each of six cellblocks, four for men and two for women. Capacity was 200 men and 80 women. There were 144 cells, each seven by ten feet in size, with a different key for each cell. Under normal conditions it took six minutes to unlock all doors in each cellblock.

Tragedy struck on February 4, 1942, because of a fire in the jail, caused by a prisoner.

Thomas Edwin Kelly, twenty-four, an aircraft worker, was booked into the jail at 3:30 a. m. that day for intoxication. Later he said he was upset because his wife left him. He was placed in a cell in the "drunk tank," but when he became unruly he was moved to a cell padded with cork, covered for sanitary purposes with roofing (tarpaper) material. He was permitted to keep his cigarettes and matches. Kelly said he tried to light a cigarette and the match head flew off and ignited the cell.

Cries of fire were heard at 4:15 a. m. and jailers found Kelly's cell in flames. The roofing paper was believed fireproof, but when strips were torn from it, it was learned later, the exposed ends were

Above: Of ninety-two San Diego policemen who served in WW2, 1st Lt. Frank E. Myrick, USAAF, DFC, was the only one killed in action. Right: Howard Roe, happily doing his duty as a juvenile division sergeant. Roe and Charles Dibb organized the Police Pals Clubs in 1940.

flammable. An earlier fire in a padded cell had been easily extinguished by jailers. Sergeant Mike Shea, in charge of the graveyard shift, opened the cell and released Kelly, and as he had done in the earlier fire, threw a bucket of water on the flames. There was an explosion. The Fire Department received a call at 4:19 a. m.

Lack of a master key proved to be deadly. Jailers and firemen battled flames and desperately tried to save the doomed men. As the prisoners in cells in the upper tier were dying, one prayed and others screamed. As soon as the fire was out, police and firemen were able to open individual cells and remove the prisoners. They found five dead and ten injured.

Kelly was charged in a complaint the same day with five counts of murder and later arraigned. John T. Holt, who was on his way to a brilliant career as a trial lawyer, told in 1986 of his part in the inquest:

"In those days we had no court-appointed attorneys for indigent prisoners, but most of us out of professional courtesy would take a defense for free. Detective Lt. Dieckmann secretly visited my office through the back door and asked me to take Kelly's case, as he believed the young man was being framed.

"I accepted the case," Holt continued. "I tried to inspect the fire scene and Chief Cliff Peterson threw me out. I got a court order for inspection and returned, to have a smiling police chief pave the way into the charred jail cell. While in the cell I managed to 'preserve some evidence'—get a piece of the tarpaper that was intact."

Coroner Chester Gunn presided over the inquest, and testimony was heard starting February 10. There was testimony that officials had considered installing a master-locking system for jail cells, but because of the expense this project had been tabled.

When police testified the tarpaper was fireproof, attorney Holt approached the jury and held up the piece of tarpaper he had taken from the cell. He lit a match to the exposed end and the sample exploded in his hands. Holt said the criminal case against Kelly exploded at that moment. The inquest jury's verdict: Kelly not criminally responsible for the deaths. Later all charges were dropped.

Criticism of police in their handling of prisoners and lack of regulations for ensuring safety had a lasting effect on management of the City Jail, right up to its closing thirty-two years later in 1974. Many improvements were made during these years.

After the war ended, Fred E. Edwards, an auxiliary policeman, wrote the City Council on August 25, 1945, expressing for himself and other citizens this opinion of the police: "San Diego has completed one of the most difficult periods in its entire existence. For four years, the streets have been flooded with war workers and military personnel. In becoming a boom town San Diego attracted the worst of other cities and the crime lineup has plagued this town.

"In spite of these facts the San Diego Police Department has kept the entire situation under control. The department has done an outstanding job."

The war ended in August 1945, and the Police Department abruptly entered a reorganization period that brought greater professionalism. A new tan uniform (replacing the old blues) was part of the postwar reorganization, the effective date July 1, 1947. Traffic officers had worn the tan uniform during the war. Other officers were given until the following November to make the change. New tan uniform trousers cost $20, the shirt $12.50, and the cap $5; the blue dress coat was retained. The change affected 250 officers.

Officers who were hired from 1935 through World War II have reported there was no formal training program. Despite

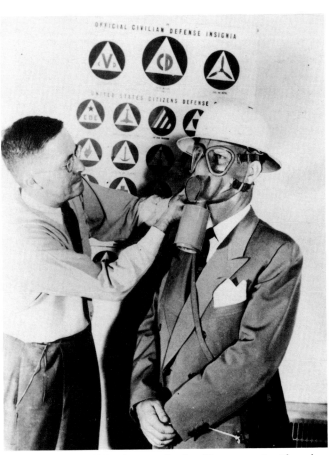

Police Lieutenant Ed Dieckmann adjusting chin strap on air raid warden gas mask worn by Officer Ken Blucher.

the advice of many experts going back to 1917, the department was still giving rookies the humiliating entrance-level routine from veterans: "I found out the hard way, now it's your turn." Some have bitter memories of their first day—drawing tarnished badges, guns with rusty plating, and, worse, getting the cold shoulder from the old-timers who believed that every rookie could be a stool pigeon for the Old Man (the chief).

Starting with Chief Peterson, a new day dawned for recruits. Chief Sears in the 1930s had some classes, with each watch captain giving his men a half-hour discussion on criminal law before shift time, but no formal training. The suddenness of the war late in 1941 smothered all hopes of formal training as manpower became acute and green hands were being hired and sent out, as of old, to fend for themselves.

Now the days of the cold shoulder were about to be replaced by a glad hand for rookies. Peterson, the technician, launched the department into the age of professionalism, but he was not to remain long enough to claim full credit. His successor, Jansen, would have to complete the job, and complete it he did.

A key figure was Walter R. Scott, a school teacher when he joined the department in 1935. With the backing of several chiefs, he single-handedly hewed out a criminal laboratory, built around a modern photographic department. Scott worked full-time in the photo lab and developed the criminal lab in spare time. He also pioneered formal training under Cliff Peterson, teaching officers part-time on various subjects. His formal classes for officers were held once or twice a year, for small groups of never more than eight men at a time, some of these being recruits and some being old-timers ambitious to better themselves.

Scott also taught fingerprint classification. He wrote a handbook, *Fingerprint Mechanics*, which was published in 1951, six years before his retirement as a lieutenant. It became a popular textbook with police departments and was followed in 1978 by *Scott's Fingerprint Mechanics* by Robert D. Olsen, Sr., a special agent in charge of the latent fingerprint division of the Army, with a foreword by Scott.

In the preface Olsen wrote this: "The book has been acknowledged as one of the most outstanding texts pertaining to fingerprinting that has ever been published. Mr. Scott's book gained wide recognition because it was practical and provided the information essential to good fingerprint work."

A new police training school was announced January 17, 1945, to teach the young officers who were replacing veteran policemen called to war service. This three-week course was under the joint direction of Scott and Sergeant Robert J. Karrow.

A little later Chief Peterson made Karrow director

Patrolman Robert Karrow (left) and Sgt. Hugh Rochefort in the target room in the new police headquarters opened in 1939.

of training. With this move Peterson set the department on its modern course, substituting professionally trained officers for hard-boiled cops who learned police work in the school of hard knocks.

Karrow recalled the moment he was put in charge of training: "I told Peterson I didn't know whether I could do it, and he said I could learn. I did, the hard way." Karrow, who had an inquisitive mind, in some ways was ahead of the times. He conducted research in police use of hypnosis, the polygraph (lie detector), and truth serums on his own time. He rejected the idea of using the serum, but insisted in the early 1950s that the polygraph and hypnosis would become valid tools for interrogation.

As training director, Karrow set up a state-accredited police school from scratch. He became possessed with the task. Peterson created a training committee that consisted of the superintendent of the San Diego Vocational School (now City College), Scott, and Karrow. Officers selected as the first instructors of the new police school were required to take a teacher training course at the vocational school. This developed part-time instructors from the ranks, and by 1947 there were two full-time and twenty part-time officer-teachers.

Those selected to teach were certificated by the state with limited credentials in their subjects. They eventually taught recruits and reserve officers. The program was enlarged through 1946 and 1947. Recruits sometimes worked thirteen hours, four in the classroom and the remainder in the field under the watchful eyes of senior officers and commanders. At first recruits were in the classroom only two months, later almost four months. All recruits who completed prescribed

courses received college credits (as they do today) which counted toward an associate in arts degree.

The department house organ *Flash* noted on March 21, 1947, that Peterson had finished seven years as chief and "has given this department the reputation all over the country of being one of the most modern and self-sufficient police machines in operation."

The *Flash* also bragged, "If you were to canvass all the police departments you would find very few that have such things as police laboratories, gymnasiums, modern identification bureaus, radio communications, specialized police photography, training schools, public relations departments, and an administrative set-up that could compare with what we have in San Diego."

But that didn't mean the department had achieved full independence from politics. Bob Karrow said it was common knowledge that Peterson resented interference from some politicians in City Hall, which led to his decision to find another job.

Peterson in 1947 angled for a newly created state position, commissioner of the California Highway Patrol. On September 29, Governor Earl Warren announced his appointment of Peterson as the first CHP commissioner at a salary of $12,000 annually. A few hours later, City Manager Fred A. Rhodes recommended Capt. Jansen, forty-four, head of the police patrol division, to fill the $7,000-a-year post that Peterson would vacate on October 15.

Cliff Peterson, the technician who started the San Diego Police Department on the road to professionalism and national recognition, died five years later of a heart ailment while serving as CHP commissioner in Sacramento.

Chapter 15
JANSEN, SUPERCHIEF

Never has there been a day at police headquarters like October 16, 1947, the day Adam Elmer Jansen became chief.

The summer days had been long as Police Chief Cliff Peterson maneuvered in Sacramento for his appointment to head the state highway patrol. It was a trying period for both Jansen and the rank and file. It was conceded that Jansen would succeed Peterson and would clean house. Peterson had failed to fill a number of vacant top posts created by retirement of captains. Lieutenants were serving as acting captains, and Jansen believed this weakened the administration.

Most of his predecessors had taken office with a low profile, playing it safe with the standard statement: "No changes." Jansen was different. He had a blueprint based on nearly sixteen years of experience on the force and a clinical study of its operation. Under Chiefs Newsom and Sears he had been department secretary, a key position. He knew what was good for the force and, after enduring a parade of chiefs in his first ten years as a policeman, knew what was bad. He wasted no time getting his show under way.

Jansen's old friend who became his top aide, Deputy Police Chief Wesley S. Sharp, recalled that first morning: "Jansen was a strict disciplinarian and everybody on the force knew it. It wasn't fear of Elmer, it was apprehension. The rank and file knew what was going to happen, and it did, real fast."

On that morning, Jansen in full uniform was busy rebuilding the force. From his desk flowed a steady stream of orders, moving officers like chessmen. In addition to filling key positions in his first general order, he was prying entrenched officers from prized assignments. Many of these found themselves

Adam Elmer Jansen. He came prepared to be chief in 1947.

by nightfall on the patrol graveyard shift.

Old-timers recalled, "Wherever you were on duty from the beginning of his administration, regardless the hour of day or night, suddenly Chief Jansen showed up, personally checking on operations."

A special bulletin issued that first day created two deputy chiefs, Lieutenant W. S. Sharp and Captain W. Elmer Warner. The ties between Jansen and these two men went back to the day when all three took the city civil service examination for appointment as rookie policemen. All three were appointed at the depth of the Depression from the same list of eligibles, Sharp and Warner on May 16, 1931, and Jansen on March 8, 1932.

Jansen was careful to explain to the press that the two new deputy chief positions he was creating followed the general recommendations outlined in a survey of the department made by the Public Administration Service of Chicago in September 1946. Sharp was given command of operations and Warner supervision of services.

His choice of Sharp as the No. 2 man was a good one. At the time, Wesley Sharp was head of the homicide squad. He and Jansen had been friends long before they joined the force. In his thirty-six years in the department, Sharp wore a uniform only four months. He held many rough assignments as a detective. The first sixteen years as an officer he had been primarily an investigator. His last twenty were in administration, in the front office.

Sharp knew the detective division inside and out. Jansen, who had worked short terms in this division, primarily was a patrol officer, and together the two men made a good administrative team. They were true collaborators.

Jansen's first bulletin made it clear that some of the past abuses and petty dishonesty would not be tolerated. The practice of using department cars and motorcycles for personal use was discontinued, immediately. Only specifically authorized vehicles could be used. "Do not ask for a car unless on business," Jansen ordered. The regulation on use of cars was the result of "a dozen or fifteen members of the department driving cars home at night," Jansen told the press. This set a pattern for his long administration as a no-nonsense chief who believed in old-fashioned honesty. He also put all officers attached to divisions other than detective, crime prevention, or maintenance work in uniform when on duty.

In his first order he assigned four lieutenants, all soon to be promoted to captain, to head the divisions of patrol, traffic, detectives, and substations. In a later order Jansen picked other men for promotion who for years to come would form the backbone of the department. Many would serve the city well and faithfully for years after he was gone. They were proud to call themselves "Jansen men," men who had worked for "the superchief."

Sergeant Dave Allsbrook expressed the general feeling of the men in the ranks when Jansen became chief: "We really started to look towards professionalization. A new department manual was developed and issued, and intensive training began. Jansen completely reorganized the department, streamlined operations and enforced strict discipline. Equipment improved. The Police Officers Association asked the City Council for better working conditions and benefits, which improved morale and made the job of being a policeman more attractive. Applications for appointment to the force at times exceeded 300."

World War II bequeathed new problems to the San Diego police. The construction of Linda Vista for wartime housing was the opening wedge for expansion that spread to all of Kearny Mesa and to the east and north. The city population leveled off at 280,000 after the war, but the tide of sailors continued as the Navy expanded bases. The 1950 census set the population at 334,387.

Postwar problems included the population explosion and an accompanying increase in the crime rate; housing expansion with increased demands on patrol; an increasing number of tourists; and the sudden mobility offered by unrationed gasoline and new autos, which in turn led to creation of the freeway system and regional shopping centers.

One of the best insights into Elmer Jansen appeared in an interview by Lionel Van Deerlin, then a staff writer for the *San Diego Journal*, later a congressman:

He was hesitant, a slow-smiling hulk of a man with a thick-set face revealing the near-straight German ancestry despite a Danish name. A great team man, he insists all police activity requires the participation of many men.

The new chief lives alone in a bachelor apartment, an astonishingly neat place he rented new twelve years ago. He cooks breakfast for himself, eats other meals out. [An earlier marriage ended in divorce. Jansen had a married daughter living in Los Angeles. These facts he jealously guarded as personal matters.]

The new chief has engaged in gunfire just twice. "Shooting is hardly ever necessary," Jansen says, "and the man who tells you he shoots to wound is crazy. My rule is don't shoot unless you're justified in killing."

The *Union* said Jansen had a "steel-trap mind" and described him as "an officer who has made it his business to know the rules," adding, "a normally silent, businesslike fellow, often to the point of taciturnity, he has no comment to make on his appointment. Of one thing you may be certain, to put it in the idiom of a veteran of many years on the police force: 'He's one of the squarest, smartest cops I've ever seen. You'll know you've got a chief of police.'"

He was born in Saint Paul, Minnesota, in 1903, and as a boy went with his parents to Panama, where his father was an engineer in the canal construction. From Central America the family moved to an Escondido ranch. When grown, he went to work for Richfield Oil Company in San Diego. As the Depression deepened, he was district credit manager, with more title than salary. Steady employment and retirement benefits lured him into the Police Department. Before joining the police, he moonlighted on weekends as a deputy sheriff at the San Ysidro border. He was twenty-nine when appointed to the force on March 8, 1932. From that day, his ambition was to become chief, and, after a remarkable rise through the ranks, at forty-four he became the twenty-fifth chief at an annual salary of $7,044.

Jansen had little patience for sycophants or parasites in the ranks and could quickly spot a bad apple in his troops. He was an administrator with an uncanny sense for the malingerer, as many were to discover over the years. A close observer of the many chiefs he had served under, he instinctively recognized behavior patterns revealing the good and the bad among personnel.

He was a stickler for efficiency and loyalty, and if economy cut into efficiency, he balked. Jansen insisted his men tell the truth. He developed a quick and sure grasp of people and their problems. He had a keen eye and nose for detail. He could smile easily, but the smile could be deceptive. Few officers were comfortable in his presence, but all knew they were lucky to have him as a leader. Jansen had a wry sense of humor and a genuine liking for horseplay, but it had to be in its place.

He demanded loyalty, and got it, because loyalty to him was a two-way street. Men in the ranks always knew where their chief stood. One expressed it well: "If Jansen told you to do something, then for better or worse he backed you all the way."

He remained for all his years a field officer, an unpredictable leader who often appeared in the middle of the night at the station. He was ever prompt in his personal thanks to

Left: Gerald H. Martindale works the police radio console in the business office created late in 1947. Right: Police and lifeguards shared this building at Santa Monica Avenue and Abbott Street in Ocean Beach, erected in the 1930s as a Works Progress Administration project. This substation and the one in East San Diego were closed by Chief Jansen.

an officer who served with distinction; let one of them stumble and he swiftly showed his displeasure.

Jansen never had a press officer and did not need one—he was the public relations man, enjoying the added duty. First, he had an inherent sense of fairness to the press. If a complaint by a representative of the news media was valid, Jansen did not hesitate to take corrective action. If the complaint was without merit, the media person who made it received a lecture which he or she never forgot. Jansen did not know the words "No comment." He had one consistent answer to media inquiries which touched on politics: "I think you better ask District Attorney Don Keller that question. He's elected and I'm appointed."

Jansen left a record difficult for any historian to abstract. It was a steady, unending drive for perfection.

During the many years he was chief, the city was a "closed town," as it has continued to be. Once asked by a reporter if "curbstone" bookmakers (little operators doing business on the street) fitted in with a closed town, he said he did not have the budget or manpower to suppress that form of petty gambling and it wasn't worth it, but he did close down the race wire and stopped organized gambling.

A modern, comprehensive manual of operations, an update of rules and operations, was one of Jansen's first orders of business, and he got it promptly. He called Robert Karrow, who remained as training officer, and ordered the manual. Karrow had worked for months on a new one, which was already written. Jansen asked to see it, thumbed through it, and handed it back, saying, "Print it."

"Just like that," Karrow recalled. He added: "This was a critical time for the force, when we moved from muscle to

brains. Peterson was the technician; Jansen the policeman. Before them, no effort had been made toward making a policeman a respected professional or even a trained employee. What has been since Jansen has largely been refinements."

When Jansen became chief there were, in the opinion of many, three separate police departments—patrol, traffic, and detectives. Each of these divisions received from the central telephone switchboard inquiries pertaining to their individual assignments, and they dispatched their own units. This sometimes led to confusion and duplication, and was often believed a throwback to the obsolete desk sergeant system of dispatching.

Making it his first priority in reorganization to put communications under one command, Jansen established a modern central business office and communications system.

Jansen built his administration upon the patrol division, in which he included traffic officers. This division was the most important in crime prevention, he believed, and the patrol division is still in fact considered the leader in the war on crime. He lectured detectives who were hogging all the glory on cases made at night by hard-working patrolmen who then the next day too often heard detectives taking unearned credit for the arrests.

Of all he did, Jansen would later say: "You can't set me up as an original thinker. The ideas we used we borrowed from others, adapting them for our own use. In some cases I think we made improvements."

The police school became an academy in 1949. San Diego City College began to offer an associate in arts degree in police science, and in-service voluntary training was given to veteran officers, an idea which proved popular. Jansen also established a policy of training recruits for suburban city police departments at the police academy. Graduating officers from different departments would work side by side throughout the county, all with the same training.

In 1954 Jansen announced that policewomen would be recruited to work in prescribed civilian clothing in detective division assignments. This revived a city civil service police rating which had existed in 1926 but which had been abolished in an economy move in 1939. Jansen was the first chief to appoint a policewoman in more than fourteen years.

The years of Jansen's administration passed swiftly, and he marked each anniversary in October with a special "commanding officers" dinner at the police pistol range. His eighth anniversary dinner in 1955 was one of special celebration, to mark his achievement of one of his long-held ambitions—to be the chief to hold the office longest. In that

On July 1, 1954 four policewomen were appointed, the first since the mid-1920s. By mid-July, 1969, the ranks had swelled to nine, shown here. Seated, left to right, Barbara Lou Allen, Sally Peterson, Molly Martin, and Marilyn Sunday Donnelly. Standing, left to right, Bernice Slunaker Caswell, Connie Van Patton, Sandra Fields, Adrienne Parson Casey, and Tommy Powell. Allen and Donnelly were two of the first four appointed in 1954. Today there are 244 policewomen on the force.

year he had bested the tenure of Chief Patrick (eight years and 110 days), and Jansen was to serve another six years, setting a record of fourteen years as top cop, a record which remains unbroken.

Those first eight years he served as chief were crucial. The growth of San Diego in all ways was phenomenal. Demands upon the department were tremendous, and Jansen maintained high standards in meeting the challenge. He zealously sought to better the Police Department and to help the general cause of all law enforcement, serving as president of the California Peace Officers Association and on the Governor's Advisory Committee on Law Enforcement.

In the first ten years of his administration the department grew to 609 officers and 95 civilians, covering 153 square miles from Del Mar to San Ysidro. The population had passed the half-million mark. The police budget swelled to $4.3 million and the police chief's salary increased to $1,160 a month. Department strength remained fairly constant at 1.15 per 1,000 population, with 3.76 officers per square mile.

Jansen by 1957 had achieved one of his goals, abolishing

two of the substations. "The basic reason was we didn't need the Ocean Beach or East San Diego stations any more," he said later. "Better communications and techniques had weakened their importance. I thought also of closing the La Jolla station, but didn't."

Jansen moved to establish a new border substation at San Ysidro and a police checkpoint at the Mexican border gate. It served to screen juveniles going into Mexico and turn back those who were unescorted. He improved liaison with Tijuana law enforcement agencies.

In 1951 he achieved a 40-hour week for the force. He created beach patrols to handle special crowds and to focus when needed on certain crimes. At the insistence of City Manager George Bean, he implemented a transition from two-man patrol cars to cars with only one officer, a move to use manpower more efficiently

The San Diego Police Reserve program was established on the orders of Chief Jansen in the summer of 1950. The reserve officers were an outgrowth of the World War II civil defense system, which trained a corps of civilians to deal with the confusion that would follow a bombing or natural disaster. The program had changed radically since the original conception when civilians, called "auxiliary officers," were used to replace regular police. When the war ended they were disbanded, only to be reactivated for the Korean War. It wasn't until 1958 that the organization began to take its present form: members became uniformed police reserves, received regular training at the academy, and were molded into a first-class law enforcement unit that saves the city thousands of dollars yearly.

Karrow, the department training officer, gives credit to early contributions to the program by banker Tom Sefton, "Bucky" Harris, Sid Lehman, Sam Urban, and Vernon Smith. "The reserve officers represented all walks of life—a banker, broker, merchant, cook, truck driver, laborer and supervisor," Karrow recalled.

In 1967 the California Penal Code was amended to include the reserves as peace officers while on active duty. So far had we come from the days of 1912 and the anonymous vigilantes. Reserve officers provide their own uniforms, work without pay, and assist regular police in many functions.

The Law Enforcement Code of Ethics was written by a group of San Diego officers headed by Captain Gene Muehleisen. First appearing early in the 1960s, it was adopted by the California Peace Officers Association and became the code of many police agencies across the nation. Later, Muehleisen became head of POST, the state of California's Police Officers Standards and Training Office.

Another step toward greater professionalism was the decision by the San Diego Police Officers Association to discontinue, after nearly fifty years, the annual police ball. The annual balls were money-makers, generating a yearly revenue averaging $15,000, but many citizens complained about being "sandbagged" to buy tickets.

After Screen Gems (Columbia Pictures) began producing the popular syndicated television series "Manhunt," starring Victor Jory as a San Diego police detective lieutenant, the production company paid $15,000 to the SDPOA in 1959 and again in 1960. With this windfall in its treasury, the association discontinued the balls. The television series ceased production at the end of 1960, but the policemen's balls were not revived.

On Christmas Day, 1955, Jansen married Captain Frances Blumfeld of the Los Angeles County Sheriff's

Above: Two San Diego policemen check out a car during a riot of hot rod dragsters on El Cajon Boulevard in East San Diego, August 22, 1960. Below: At the entrance of City Jail, 801 West Market Street, prisoners are being loaded for arraignment at the County Courthouse.

Left: A paddy wagon prisoner break is re-enacted, March 25, 1958.
Above: This is an aerial view of the Southern Division police station near
the International Border at San Ysidro, opened in 1962, first of the
modern division headquarters, which by 1989 numbered seven.

Office, in a ceremony in Yuma, Arizona. It was the second marriage for each. At the time of the marriage Frances Jansen was in charge of the women's division of the Los Angeles County Jail and had been a sheriff's officer for thirteen years. They met at a convention and their romance led to a lasting marriage. She took a leave of absence and later resigned her position to move with Jansen to a home they bought on Mount Helix.

After twenty-nine years and ten months as a police officer, Jansen retired early in 1962 upon being appointed San Diego County Sheriff, succeeding Bert Strand, seventy, who was quitting after serving twenty years. The appointment to fill out the unexpired term was effective January 8, 1962, with an annual salary of $19,800.

Jansen's police administration was summarized on August 3, 1962, in an article by Ralph Bennett, political writer of the *Tribune*: "Open prostitution and bookmaking were closed down and kept closed. Traffic tickets could not be fixed. Officers maintained high standards of conduct or were punished swiftly and severely. The department got a reputation for honesty and efficiency. Morale soared. The crime rate stayed low."

The sheriff's appointment brought Jansen for the first

time in his law enforcement career face to face with the electorate. He had to run for a full four-year term against Police Chief Joseph C. O'Connor of El Cajon. In the November general election Jansen was rated as the favorite by all news media, but the electorate had different ideas. O'Connor won, with 159,701 votes to Jansen's 156,614, and Jansen said he would not run for office again: "Once is enough."

Jansen then retired from public life. With his wife and their dogs, he went on fishing trips and worked daily on his one-acre plot of lime trees. He remained as outspoken as ever, but rarely left the "ranch." After suffering two strokes, he died on September 29, 1978, at age seventy-five.

Jansen served under four city managers. His last "boss," City Manager Tom Fletcher, once said: "A police chief is more than just an administrator, policy maker, disciplinarian and leader. It is a difficult job that few men can really do well. Chief Jansen personifies the very best in his field. I have never seen Chief Jansen hesitate in doing what he felt was right, regardless of the consequences."

Jansen, who commanded respect as few chiefs ever did, will be remembered in the history of the city as the architect of a modern metropolitan police department.

Chapter 16
THE SHARP SIXTIES

Wesley S. Sharp, who had been a capable deputy chief in charge of operations for fourteen years, was reluctant to take the top job, but was convinced by City Manager Tom Fletcher and Jansen to assume leadership. The appointment was effective January 8, 1962. Sharp, sixty-four, was a tall, bespectacled man with mostly gray hair, soft-spoken and shy, and was generally known as a low-keyed, stern administrator. He had avoided the limelight and reporters found little in the files about him.

This quiet man presided over the department during the most turbulent decade since the end of World War II.

Although born in Los Angeles, Sharp considered himself a lifelong San Diegan, as he was an infant when his parents moved to the city. His father for many years operated a livery stable. Wesley was reared in Logan Heights and was a graduate of Logan Elementary School and San Diego High School. As a youth he was interested in baseball and was remembered by his fans as a fine first baseman and catcher, and was once a major league prospect who played semipro ball. In his brief hitch in the Army Coast Artillery at Fort Rosecrans during World War I, he was captain of the battery baseball team. After school he went to work for the Standard Oil Company in San Diego and rose from driver to salesman. During the Depression, friends on the Police Department convinced him it was time to join. In competition with nearly five hundred applicants taking the city Civil Service Commission tests, Sharp finished among the top ten. Appointed May 16, 1931, he got his only training by means of the advice of older officers. He walked a downtown beat for four months, and for the rest of his career was in investigative or administrative positions.

Like officers across the nation, San Diego police had always controlled the streets by force, yet were obeyed and respected. They had the full support of citizens regardless of what action was deemed necessary. Now, suddenly, in the administration of Wesley Sharp all this was to change.

Change came in the Sixties. Respect for authority weakened. For some Americans, violence became a way of life. But the San Diego Police Department, under experienced leadership, was prepared to handle trouble without undue fuss. "We began those times with a clear, disciplined, corruption-free department enjoying a national reputation for honesty and restraint, something few other cities could lay the most oblique claim to," the 1981 SDPD commemorative album recalled.

Sharp knew San Diego and its people, way of life, and politics. He saw many changes in the city, from the relaxed morale and token law enforcement to closing of bawdy houses and relentless prosecution. Police work had become a science since his rookie days. Sharp built his own reputation as top cop. When he took over in 1962, he had 692 sworn officers and 128 civilians. Morale was high. The city's population was more than 600,000 and climbing. He could honestly say no changes were planned and everything was fine.

For his No. 2 man he selected Athos E. Sada, who had been serving as a deputy chief. Sada was a native of San Diego and son of an old friend of Sharp's, and observers said he was a cinch to be the next chief.

The Police Department could take pride in crime statistics at the time Sharp took control. The 1962 yearly crime increase was less than the national average. The August 1965 issue of *American Cities* magazine declared San Diego to be the second-safest city in the nation.

One of Sharp's first moves was to crack down on rowdy students who in past years had swarmed to San Diego beaches from all over Southern California to celebrate Easter Week vacation, creating near-riot conditions. Expected visitors in 1962 were warned police would heavily patrol all beaches. "They were going to make our beaches another Fort Lauderdale or a Palm Springs," Sharp recalled.

"But we were waiting for them. We put traffic officers in the beach area and cited students for every violation in the book. We had other officers ready to respond. The offenders went to jail, pronto. They got sick of it quick." Beach areas experienced no serious police problems in 1962, and none in the years that followed.

Late in 1962 a new substation building was completed in San Ysidro for the Southern Division at 663 Tijuana Boulevard, close to the international border. The division was created in 1958 when San Diego annexed twenty-two square miles along the border, creating South San Diego. The station provided space for one hundred officers and had complete garage facilities manned by an auto serviceman.

In the early 1960s court decisions eroded the powers of the police and, by the middle of the decade, decisions by state and federal courts had forced San Diego police to change some practices anchored in the past. Chief Sharp said these decisions hampering police were a constant source of frustration to law enforcement, "yet the Police Department has rolled with the blows."

He believed law enforcement had to improve investigative and interrogative methods, increase preventive measures, and devise favorable new techniques in community and human relations. He credited police ability to maintain a low crime rate under such adverse conditions to the higher quality of officers recruited and to the incentives for veteran policemen to continue their college studies.

Recognizing the need for improving community relations, Sharp assigned a captain to make a study as the first step in establishing a community relations program for the Police Department. The program was then established and by 1964 all officers were urged to assist in the new program, which was beginning to pay dividends.

"We face sociological problems sometimes manifested by mass civil disobedience and the threat of mob violence," Sharp told the troops. "Control of

Wesley S. Sharp. He led the department in the insolent 1960s.

these new conditions will require strict discipline. This department has shown it can bring such conditions under control with a minimum of effort, without exercising excessive force."

Lieutenant Homer Johnson and Sergeant Bill Kolender were the first full-time officers assigned to community relations. They concentrated on visits to universities, colleges and secondary schools to explain local law enforcement. When Johnson was forced to retire because of illness, Kolender was promoted to lieutenant and put in charge of the ever-expanding community relations program, which by the early 1970s had a staff of ten officers with a captain in command, all especially trained.

This was police work with a contemporary slant. But Sharp's first crisis was to be a shoot-out of the old-fashioned kind, involving the biggest gun battle ever in downtown San Diego.

The shoot-out occurred on April 8, 1965, at the Hub Pawnshop on Fifth Avenue at F Street. It led to the formation of San Diego's first SWAT (Special Weapons and Tactics) team. The siege began when Robert P. Anderson, twenty-eight, a berserk laborer and known drug user, managed to load a rifle while in the shop as a prospective customer. He turned the gun on two employees, fatally wounding the manager, Lewis Richards, sixty-one. The other employee saved his life

by running upstairs, where he hid throughout the ensuing shoot-out, which lasted nearly four hours.

Anderson had at his disposal in the pawnshop twenty-seven rifles, fifty pistols, and unlimited ammunition, some of which he used against sixty-five uniformed and plainclothes officers on the street outside. Police figured they fired eight hundred rounds from revolvers, rifles, shotguns and a machine gun in their attempts to dislodge the barricaded gunman. Near the end, after tear gas was ineffective because of shifting high winds, Navy concussion grenades were used to end the siege.

Robert Crandall, fifty-two, editor of the *Independent* newspaper, while covering the story dropped dead of a heart attack. The only police casualty was Sergeant Sam Chasteen, who suffered a forehead wound when struck by an undetermined object.

A crowd estimated at a thousand risked ricocheting bullets and stood in heavy rain throughout the siege. City meter maids continued to write overtime parking tickets nearby, and mail was delivered in the area. In the end, officers stormed the upper floor, where Sergeant A. D. Brown risked his life to wound Anderson with shotgun blasts. It was all over but the paper work.

Chief Sharp commended the officers who were under fire and singled out Inspector Wayne Colburn, who commanded the operation, as well as Sergeant Brown, Sergeant "Swede" Svidal, Patrolman Robert Augustine, and Detective Lieutenant Clarence Myers. (After his retirement Colburn became a U. S. marshal, and went on to become national director of the federal marshals service.)

Anderson, convicted of murder, escaped death. The California Supreme Court declared the penalty unconstitutional and set Anderson's term at life imprisonment with the possibility of parole. In 1976, after serving eleven years, he was set free.

There were two earlier shoot-outs worth recalling here, the first on January 12, 1927, at the Mission Hills home of a well-known candy manufacturer, B. G. Showley, at 1859 Fort Stockton Drive. William Smith, the gunman, was killed. As police reconstructed the case, Smith was infatuated with the

The 1965 shoot-out at the Hub Jewelry & Loan Co., Fifth Avenue and F Street, is graphically shown in these photographs. Top: Officers with pistols and shotguns converge on the beseiged pawnshop. Below: Officers using an ambulance gurney to avoid gunfire follow a crawling detective at right in an attempt to enter the shop.

Showley maid, Mrs. Eula Caldwell, a widow. After the candy maker left for his factory, Smith entered the house by asking for the maid, and found her in an upstairs room attending Mrs. Showley, who was recovering from an illness. Smith whipped out a pistol and fired four shots across the bed, wounding the maid in one lung and left leg. Mrs. Showley crawled out of bed, grabbed her son, Guy, six, and fled outside. Police were called.

Before the siege ended, every available city policeman, as well as state and county officers, were involved. Tear gas failed to dislodge Smith from the upstairs but forced him into a front bedroom, where he barricaded himself in a closet. It happened that Showley stored his ammunition in this closet and Smith used it in the shoot-out. Officers tried firing rifle shots into the ceiling below the closet. Finally an officer smashed a hole in the closet door with a fire axe. Smith, realizing he would be gunned down, came out firing at three officers in his path. He was killed by eight police bullets. Patrolman W. D. Cody suffered a shoulder wound and later received a disability retirement.

It took four months to repair the damage before the Showley family could move back into the home, riddled by hundreds of bullets.

A shoot-out involving fifty officers occurred in Linda Vista on April 28, 1954, at 7221 Linda Vista Road. Detective John J. Zemcik, at that time a juvenile bureau officer, answered a call to investigate a family argument. When he arrived he heard a woman begging a man not to shoot. It was then that he spotted Elwin "Bunny" Bunnell, a friend and a Municipal Court deputy marshal, coming across the street on a routine mission to deliver court papers.

Sensing the danger, Zemcik jumped in front of Bunnell, told him they should play it safe, and pushed him away. As he was turning, the first shotgun blast hit Bunnell in the torso and Zemcik in the back of the head and shoulders. Zemcik summoned help and went back into action. (Bunnell recovered from serious wounds. Zemcik suffered minor injuries.)

Barney A. Dennis, thirty, was wounded and forced out of the duplex apartment with tear gas. Dennis' wife, Marionna, twenty-four, whom he held at gunpoint while firing through windows and doors at police, was shot in the left thigh by her husband. Before the thirty minutes of firing was over, a crowd of several thousand rushed to the scene, hindering police action when some strayed within gunshot range.

Gun battles like these sold newspapers but, long after his retirement, Sharp was asked what had been his biggest problem during his administration. "The No. 1 problem started in 1964 with passage by Congress of the civil rights legislation. Minorities thought they had the right to do anything, and they had no respect for law and order. CORE [Congress of Racial Equality] activity was the first indication of unrest in San Diego, starting with picketing and sit-ins. It was a trou-

James Harrell leads a lost child to a reunion with an anxious mother on the boardwalk at Mission Beach, one of many police duties of summer.

CORE demonstrations resulted in a number of misdemeanor arrests in June 1964. "I had the full backing of City Manager Fletcher, who many times said publicly the first duty of police was to protect life and property, and we could use such force as necessary to accomplish this duty," Sharp recalled.

San Diego's backlash from the Los Angeles rioting of blacks in the Watts area, which resulted in thirty-five deaths and an estimated $200 million in property damage, was not long in coming. The Watts riots started on August 11, 1965, and continued through August 16. Violence started in San Diego on August 13, a Friday, and continued throughout the weekend, tapering off by Monday, August 16.

The disorders from Friday afternoon to early Monday resulted in four injuries, none serious. One policeman was hurt when hit by a rock; a market interior was destroyed by a fire bomb, and a school building was seared by kerosene poured around the exterior. Other damage included broken windows in commercial build-

blesome time and we had no precedent, for nothing on this scale of unrest had happened in fifty-three years, not since the IWW riots of 1912."

Sharp recognized the problem and didn't waste time. His street officers were not prepared for crowd control or riot situations. Homer Johnson, who had been assigned to community relations, was a commando in World War II and had a lot of military experience training officers in riot and crowd control. Sharp put Johnson in charge of a three-day special training course for all patrol officers, and this training later served them well.

This defensive tactics training program began early in the summer of 1964. The *Union* reported 560 officers completed training in the use of an ironwood baton, two feet long and weighing three pounds. Officers were taught crowd control in ten-man squads. Sharp said by the time the training was finished, riots had become one of the most serious and dangerous situations San Diego faced.

ings, some looting, and damage to many automobiles from thrown rocks. All the violence occurred in Southeast San Diego, which was sometimes called a black ghetto.

The riots could have been far more destructive if the police had not reacted quickly with a massive presence in the area and if the officers had not been well trained to handle provocation with a minimum of force and a maximum of restraint.

Patrol Inspector Colburn, from a command post set up Friday in a parking lot at Fortieth Street and Imperial Avenue, told the news media extra officers had been moved into the district. Police could see the tension building and prepared for renewed violence.

Blacks at Mountain View Park in mid-afternoon Friday started the violence, throwing objects at passing vehicles and slightly injuring three occupants. Police quickly cleared the park of loiterers and onlookers. Motorcycle officers and police cruisers zig-zagged streets where more disturbances were reported, most of them minor. Of the twenty arrests that day, a majority were for failure to disperse. By late Friday afternoon sixty officers were on special patrol. That force was later strengthened by sixty more from the night watch and fifty reserve officers. Reinforcements were massed at the police pistol range, and most remained on duty all night.

City Manager Fletcher answered critics who said police had used too much force and were inciting trouble: "We are not going to have another Los Angeles riot situation in San Diego. We are not going to keep police out of an area just because someone says it might create trouble."

Mayor Frank Curran did not believe the city had reached the point where outside help was needed. Sharp said much later: "I had nothing to fall back on, no one to back us up. The California National Guard was fully committed in Watts. In San Diego, police were on their own. If we had not been able to contain it, I don't known where we would have turned. The military refused to help us."

The chief instructed field officers, "If at any time anybody is observed looting, and commands to halt are ignored, open fire with revolvers." He felt what happened in Watts fully justified whatever it would take to keep the peace in San Diego.

To inform the public of officials' reaction to disorders, a television panel composed of civic leaders was formed, and for the first time a broadcast was carried simultaneously by the three TV stations, Channels 6, 8, and 10. In the broadcast City Manager Fletcher said flatly: "This was not a race riot. It was a lawless attack." He added that of eighty-two persons arrested during disturbances, 86 percent had police records.

The San Diego Police Officers Association publication *Fall In*, in its issue of October 1965, editorialized: "As the long hot summer draws to a close we find ourselves in the enviable position of not having had a major outbreak of violence as experienced in New York, Chicago, Atlanta, East Lansing, Omaha, and other major cities."

Midway in his administration, on May 15, 1966, Sharp marked his thirty-fifth year on the force. He was then sixty-seven, and each year after his sixty-fifth birthday automatically had been given a written renewal by City Manager Fletcher, required of employees sixty-five or older.

Department strength grew fast in the 1960s, with sworn officers totaling more than seven hundred. In 1967, when the state Penal Code was amended to include reserves as police officers while on active duty, San Diego's reserve had blossomed into an organization of more than two hundred men, who by 1962 were contributing more than forty thousand hours yearly.

During this period the appearance of street officers changed, with an emphasis on practicality over formality. Short-sleeved shirts were worn between July 1 and October 31, and safety helmets were worn at all times instead of soft caps for patrolmen and sergeants.

Officer John Lewis wears safety helmet as he holds the cap it replaced in 1963. At right, John Morrison, member of the color guard, ca. 1970s. Below: Police Boys Band, 1965-66.

The internal investigations program was organized by Sharp in June 1967, an important move because there had previously been no particular system of keeping records of complaints concerning officers and department policies. Investigations were made by various commanding officers. Sharp assigned Lieutenant Ralph Davis to head the program, with a sergeant as assistant. They reported directly to the police chief, investigating and recording all activity. The program was successful and well accepted by officers. It was the forerunner of what later was called inspection and control.

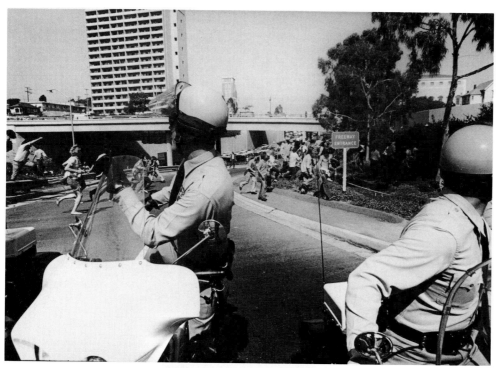

In the mid-1960s and extending into the next decade, anti-Vietnam War protesters took to the streets and into City Hall in San Diego. At left, police surveillance of a freeway entrance about to be blocked. Below, the protest is a sit-down during a City Council meeting. Opposite page top: That barren land behind the newly opened Northern Division police station on Eastgate Mall west of Genesee Avenue, shown in this 1971 photograph, is the site of today's bustling business and commercial center, the Golden Triangle in northeast La Jolla. This was the second of the modern divisional police stations built.

As policing advanced from a vocation to a profession in the 1960s, so did the tools. The one with the greatest impact was the computer. It was Sharp who launched the computer age for San Diego police in February 1965. He created a three-man team, realizing that computers might revolutionize many procedures. He put in charge Lieutenant Jack Baker, head of the record bureau, with Sergeant Robert Ristau and Patrolman John Lewis (later lieutenant) to round out the detail.

Up to this time, all criminal cases had been recorded on punched cards. The three officers attended schools conducted by a computer manufacturer that was leasing a system to the city. They reported that computers could be used in research, planning, field operations, traffic citations, and record systems.

From this modest beginning San Diego police took an early lead. In 1970, then-Congressman Lionel Van Deerlin testified before a House judiciary subcommittee that San Diego police were about two years ahead of the rest of the nation in use of computers. The system was upgraded many times in the years that followed.

Chief Sharp's most painful crisis was a personnel decision. On January 3, 1967, he summarily dismissed his protégé, Deputy Police Chief Athos E. Sada, the No. 2 man, a veteran of more than twenty-five years. In a statement announcing the dismissal, Sharp said: "I have become increasingly aware of Chief Sada's inability to administer within the department." Reasons given were lack of confidence, Sada's berating of other policemen, and conduct unbecoming an officer of his rank by being involved in a fistfight with a civilian in a

Hillcrest area restaurant. Later it was revealed that Sharp had first asked Sada to take retirement; Sada had at first agreed but then reconsidered. City Manager Walter Hahn backed Sharp in the dismissal.

Sada appealed to the City Council and city Civil Service Commission, but he changed his mind and submitted his resignation February 19.

When it came time to retire (he was past his sixty-ninth birthday), Sharp did it quietly and without fanfare, in a manner typical of his more than thirty-six years as a policeman. He issued a short statement that it was time to move along. He said he was leaving a force that was in good hands. It had been a pleasure to be associated with clean and efficient city government. He added, "Few citizens realize how important an honest city administration is to their safety and enjoyment of life."

When he retired on January 2, 1968, he had more years on the force than any chief before him. His counsel was sought by every chief who served after him into the 1980s. Detective A. K. Wood summarized how officers felt on Sharp's last anniversary as chief when he told the top cop: "You haven't advanced much in the last twenty years, you've only been promoted once—to chief."

Sharp in retirement remained active in civic affairs. He died December 3, 1991, in a San Diego convalescent home, age ninety-three. At the memorial service, Police Chief Robert Burgreen said Wes Sharp was the last strong link between the past and present of the department, a man who loved the force and whose counsel throughout the years had strengthened and nurtured it.

Above: "Neither rain, nor sleet, nor snow"…Well, let's say only rain in San Diego could keep this patrolman from his appointed rounds when his patrol car stalled in flooded Market Street in front of police headquarters. The officer was Robert Slaughter and the year 1968.

Chapter 17
ROED'S ROUGH ROAD

In announcing Sharp's retirement, City Manager Walter Hahn, Jr., said he would ask the City Council to confirm his appointment of Deputy Chief O. J. Roed as Sharp's successor. This the council was quick to do.

Jimmy Roed (pronounced "road") had administrative training to prepare him for the job—eleven years in the investigative division (five as chief of detectives). But he had less than two years in the front office and lacked experience in the patrol and traffic divisions.

The day after his appointment, a fellow officer told him: "Jim, you sure haven't had a very stable position here. You've had three different jobs in a year." Roed had been promoted from chief of detectives to assistant chief in charge of services on October 28, 1966, and on April 11, 1967, succeeded Sada as deputy chief. Roed was forty-eight when he became the top policeman and was a veteran of more than twenty-seven years on the force. Yet as chief he would last only three years.

Jimmy—six feet one inch, blue eyes, slim—was an avid golfer. The police commemorative album in 1981 gave this word picture: "We began those years with a clean, disciplined, corruption-free department enjoying a national reputation for honesty and restraint. Our new chief was Olif J. Roed, a brisk and energetic father-figure. We liked it when he arrived on the scene of a demonstration gone awry, often as not in faded khaki pants and a baseball cap, his golf clubs over his shoulder, telling us to stay calm, that he'd be with us until it was over. We liked the personally signed letters of congratulations; the smiling, unplanned appearances at lineups; and here and there even a card for the birth of a son or daughter, signed 'Mr. and Mrs. O. J. Roed.'"

From the point of view of the rank and file, Jimmy was a nice guy, a good leader who backed his troops to the hilt. He had served as the president of the Police Officers Association.

His father, Olaf, a native of Norway, died a year after he was born, and his mother, Minnie, a nurse and governess, raised him. The difference in spelling—Olaf for his father and Olif for the son—was the result of a birth certificate error that was never corrected. Jimmy was born and educated in San Diego. His first taste of being a lawman was during a summer vacation when he was fourteen, patrolling the corridors of the old downtown library as a security guard. He met his wife, Nellie, a tall, pretty brunette, in a dairy where they both worked. They were married in May 1941. He had taken the police examination at the urging of his mother and won appointment as a rookie. Like others before him, he served in the uniform patrol only six months before becoming a juvenile bureau detective. Jim served in the Navy in Alaska, on military leave from the department, and resumed his police career after the war.

When he took over the helm, the insolent Sixties were far from over. San Diego police took on, one by one, full-scale disturbances, campus demonstrations, and street marches, dealing with the Black Panthers and other radical groups.

Three months after he became chief, Roed told members of the local American Civil Liberties Union that he and officers of the force faced many problems, including recruitment and retention of officers, a rising crime rate, the uneasiness of law-abiding citizens, narcotics and drug abuse, adverse court decisions, and the public's blaming police "for every social evil on the books." He linked recruitment and retention problems with the widespread view that being a policeman was a "very unattractive career."

In Roed's first year as chief, City Manager Hahn asked and was given council authority to raise the authorized department strength to 835 sworn officers, making a total of 1,028 personnel, an increase of 35 percent. Closure of the City Jail made jailers available for other assignments, as the county assumed custody of all city prisoners in the County Jail.

The 1970 census put the city's population at 696,760 and San Diego became the fourteenth largest city in the nation. Police had 327 square miles to cover with a budget of almost $13 million. The city reported 1.33 officers per thousand people and 2.99 officers per square mile.

But at times it seemed there would never be enough troops to cover all the outbreaks. A mob at the University of California at San Diego smashed windows. Black Panthers clashed with Brown Berets. The mood of the youthful participants was unpredictable, and many officers suffered a kind of battle fatigue.

The 1981 police commemorative album recalled the period: "They had gone from pounding a beat to fighting a riot in too little time, and could not be blamed if they seemed to be in shock. They were confused, tired, frustrated, bloody and harangued from all sides. The cops were suddenly underdogs."

By the end of Roed's administration the stress and strain took a toll on police, from Chief Roed on down to the walking beat man.

Roed was conscious that Chiefs Jansen and Sharp had enjoyed the fullest support from the city managers under whom they served. Unfortunately, friction developed early between Roed and City Manager Hahn. The chief believed he had been promised more pay and felt the city manager was stalling. (He started at $17,000 yearly.) So almost from the beginning there was conflict and loss of confidence. "I think under a different city manager I would have remained chief for a good many years," Roed said later.

After retirement, Roed often referred to his administration as "those rough years." The year he took office, the state attorney general and the San Diego County district attorney were engaged in a comprehensive joint investigation into allegations that officers of the San Diego police vice squad had accepted bribes and detectives of the pawnshop detail had taken gifts.

This probe, which began as a result of a 1967 Internal Revenue Service investigation into interstate transactions involving bookmaking, lasted two years and was damaging to the morale of the entire department. In addition to many civilians, a total of eighty-five officers, including Roed, were questioned. Seven police officers either retired or resigned, and others were criticized by state investigators for refusing to cooperate.

The investigation resulted in an explosive report which District Attorney Don Keller refused to release. Keller told the news media he believed it was filled with "innuendoes and half-truths." The final draft, which was delivered to City Manager Hahn on January 23, 1970, included this statement: "This investigation developed no evidence to indicate corruption involving present members of the San Diego Police Department. Prosecutable wrongdoing uncovered occurred entirely beyond the statute of limitations. For this reason, no criminal actions have resulted." Both the city administration and the police said the 23-page report was not documented and simply "rehashed rumors."

Thus ended what Chief Roed had, at various times during the joint probe, termed "a witch hunt." City Manager Hahn found no basis for disciplinary action within the Police Department but later issued a new city "code of ethics," requiring city employees to cooperate fully with judicial bodies and lawfully constituted investigative commissions. This was a

Chief O. Jimmy Roed. He was a brisk, energetic father-figure.

response to the fact that some officers had invoked their constitutional right against self-incrimination in refusing to answer questions about possible corruption.

In retrospect, Roed's corrosive years began with the annoyance and morale problem this joint probe created, and continued until his disability retirement. He could find comfort in the highly competent commanding officers he gathered around him, who were completely loyal when the time came to choose between their chief and the city manager. Jimmy's first year in office held much promise, but he did not have the opportunity to formulate policies before the feud developed with City Manager Hahn, a man of chilly and remote demeanor.

Hahn, throughout his tenure as city manager, was known to colleagues as a conscientious professional who did a competent job. Those who worked closely with him considered him a tough, hard-working administrator who demanded much from the staff. Hahn, who had succeeded Tom Fletcher as manager in October 1966, believed the city government was doing a good job and tried to contribute his part.

Early in the chief's administration, civil rights leaders pressured Roed to promote minorities to sergeant or higher positions on the force in community relations without going through the city Civil Service Commission. Roed reacted quickly, calling all black patrolmen to a conference. The black officers told the chief they would refuse promotion to sergeant if not made on merit and qualified and certified by the commission. Finally the commission approved the creation of two new community relations positions that reported to the chief of police, with the same salary range as a police sergeant. One of these spots was promptly filled with a black.

Civil disorders continued to sweep over the nation every summer, mostly in black urban neighborhoods, but did not recur in San Diego until May 11, 1969, when trouble erupted again in Mountain View Park in Southeast San Diego. It was Jimmy Roed's misfortune that the riot that then occurred and its aftermath in the city administration would deepen the mistrust between his office and that of the city manager, and would be the beginning of the end of his term.

The Mountain View Park troubles had been building for months. As Roed said later: "Hoodlums made it a no-man's land." The serious rioting at this park did not occur until a weekend in July, reaching its climax on a Sunday, July 13, when two people died of gunshot wounds. Sniper fire, looting, and arson broke out in the southeast section of the city in a wide-ranging disorder that was confronted by a massive concentration of police and firemen. Fire nearly destroyed one market; nineteen stores were broken into and looted, and windows were smashed in five other stores. Pistols, a rifle, and ammunition were stolen from one store.

Of the thirty people arrested, about half were juveniles. The situation became so intense that Chief Roed stationed officers on the roof and in the patio of the Market Street police headquarters. Ultimately, more than two hundred policemen were deployed in the southeast area, and tear gas and riot control sweeps with batons were used before the area was cleared and calm restored.

After this riot, which Manager Hahn attributed to "highly organized gangs," city officials vowed to protect law-abiding citizens in this area. Citizens involved presented Roed with a petition bearing two-thousand signatures. "That was an amazing document to come from that area," Roed said. "They were all blacks. They wanted more police protection."

Roed said he immediately took the petition to Hahn and requested that Mayor Frank Curran and the City Council members be notified. He said Hahn approved boosting strength to six officers in three cars, adequate to handle hoodlums prowling the park.

Ten to twelve days later Hahn took Roed into the mayor's office, where Roed realized the mayor had not been notified nor had the mayor agreed to the park plan. Curran wanted the chief to remove officers from the park and take shotguns out of cars.

"I told the city manager and the mayor removing troops from the park would be a serious mistake, but finally agreed to remove the shotguns and they agreed to continue the special park patrol."

Roed then recalled the aftermath:

The following Saturday [July 26] I was attending a seminar at a Mission Bay hotel when one of my assistant chiefs telephoned and said the city manager had called a meeting in his office of all the chief officers of the Police Department. I was not aware of this meeting and told my caller Hahn knew where I was and if he wanted me to attend, I could be there in ten minutes. I stayed at the seminar but heard nothing from Hahn. When I got home several of these staff officers called me about meeting with Hahn, and said he demanded a change in the handling of police patrols in Mountain View Park. He wanted to pull the troops out and said I opposed this. He gave them no explanation of why I was not invited to the meeting. He tried

to get support of my chief officers, going over my head, but they didn't give him support and stayed with me.

Roed said he contacted Hahn, expressing concern about the meeting and asking to see him.

He said to be at his residence in Clairemont at 8 p.m. I canceled a social engagement and arrived at Hahn's home at 8 o'clock, and found Kimball Moore and John Lockwood [both assistant city managers] there but no Hahn. He had gone to a party. I told Lockwood and Moore I didn't want to talk to them. I said I wanted to talk to Hahn and couldn't run a police operation this way and that I was quitting.

Hahn arrived about an hour later and he and I went at it hot and heavy until almost midnight. Then, after everything I had said to him, he told me he wanted me to stay on the job. "If you quit, it will cost me my job," he said.

I then said I didn't see how I could continue to serve as chief because of what I had said to him, and that if anyone talked to me the way I talked to him, I'd fire him. He replied, "Oh, no, we can forget and forgive and everything will be all right."

The meeting closed on this note, and a truce between the two men lasted almost a year. Then came another blow. Robert Jauregui had been appointed by Roed as his No. 2 man on the retirement of D. Kenneth Blucher from the post. The chief believed Jauregui, prior to the promotion, had answered to Hahn's satisfaction questions relative to Jauregui's association with Charlie Pratt, a neighbor and close friend who was former president of the Yellow Cab Company.

"Jauregui was in the No. 2 spot a month or six weeks when I started receiving rather pointed questions from Hahn about reports of favors Bob had received from Pratt on trips the two took to Las Vegas and Baja California," Roed recalled. "I kept Bob informed of this series of inquiries. He assured me these trips were taken with approval of superiors in 1966, at the time he was a captain. Over the years that had passed, the city policy and that of police on accepting gratuities changed radically, from being acceptable to not."

On March 11, 1970, Hahn ordered Roed to demote Jauregui for accepting Pratt's favors. Hahn was adamant. No police officer should accept favors even from a neighbor or friend, especially when the friend is in a business which is police-regulated, as was the cab business.

Roed termed Hahn's order "a mistake," insisting Jauregui had not violated department regulations. But nine days later he followed his boss's order, and demoted Jauregui to his former position, deputy chief. "I think Bob Jauregui suffered a grave injustice," Roed said later. "I don't know any other way to describe it. What brought this on was a flap over the Yellow Cab people offering gifts of value to the mayor and others prior to their indictments, and I felt they were getting back at Charlie Pratt." In a letter replying to Hahn's demotion order, Roed described Jauregui as "an outstanding officer whose integrity and honesty has been above reproach."

That following September the county grand jury began a full-scale investigation of Yellow Cab contributions to city, county, and state officials. This ushered the city into a new decade carrying on its back a load of bribery and conspiracy accusations as indictments were handed down by the grand jury, naming Mayor Curran, Deputy Mayor Alan Hitch, and seven other city officials. This stemmed from the testimony of Pratt before the grand jury that a 1967 rate hike had been granted his cab company with the aid of under-the-counter payments. Mayor Curran was found innocent of these charges in August 1971, and most of the other indictments were dismissed.

Jauregui went on to serve on the chief's staff until he had thirty years on the force, and he took his retirement in January 1976.

There was still another rough spot in Roed's road. "Hahn called me at home and said he had received a threatening phone call. I went immediately to his home and gave him my loaded revolver. I told him to use the gun if anyone intruded. I had placed a plainclothes officer on guard at his house.

"Hahn had no idea who had made the call, but said it could have been a policeman. I was concerned. There was a lot of hard feeling on the force after Jauregui's demotion. Hahn didn't request a wiretap, but I wanted one because I thought it was a policeman who had made the call. I told Officer Ken O'Brien [a lieutenant in charge of the police intelligence unit] to put a tap on the manager's home phone."

The next day [March 5, 1970] O'Brien called the chief and said, "We got caught." Hahn had not been able to call out on his phone and had complained to the phone company, which found the instrument tapped. "I told O'Brien if he was asked, I ordered the tap and I did it because I was concerned about Hahn's welfare," Roed said. This was on a weekend.

On Monday, Hahn held a press conference, reported his phone had been tapped without his permission, and said he had asked a county grand jury investigation. Roed told District Attorney Keller his side of the wiretap story. Keller presented indictments to the grand jury charging Roed, O'Brien, and Sergeant Richard Davis (who had been working with O'Brien) with illegal wiretapping. The grand jury refused to indict.

With an awkward smile for newspaper photographers, Chief Roed tenders his resignation to City Manager Walter Hahn.

Despite all the problems of this administration, many improvements were made. The Market Street police headquarters building, after thirty years, was given a $886,000 modernization in 1969. A $465,700 police and fire facility was opened on October 15, 1971, in the Golden Triangle area in northeast La Jolla, providing a new substation for the Northern Division. The post of police public information officer was established. The "Ride Along" program, with citizens invited to ride with policemen in patrol cars, was started and soon became popular.

Roed's emotional and physical troubles resulted in his being hospitalized twice, the second time in March 1971. On the advice of his physician, he decided to retire. "I had the feeling the Charlie Pratt matter, the Yellow Cab indictments against Mayor Curran and the councilmen, all had to have something to do with Hahn's attitude."

On the day Jauregui was demoted, Roed, with Hahn's approval, had appointed Raymond Hoobler to the No. 2 position. "I gave Hoobler what I thought was good advice, if he was chosen to replace me. I told him the last two years had been horrible, terrible, and that he would be working for the same boss—Hahn." Roed said Hoobler made no comment.

Roed went on sick leave on March 11, 1971, and Hoobler was named chief to replace him. Roed asked for disability retirement because of a heart ailment. The city denied him a disability retirement pension, which would be tax-free, because a city doctor found Roed suffered from hypertension but the condition was not disabling. The wrangling over this issue went on for eight months while Roed drew full pay. Finally on January 19, 1972, a state workmen's compensation referee ruled Roed was disabled by the heart ailment and entitled to disability benefits.

The "brisk father-figure" who became chief in 1968 was a frustrated veteran when he stepped down, still deeply concerned for the police force in which he had fierce pride.

As long as he was chief he had a little sign on a little table next to his desk. It read, "EMPATHY," and in smaller letters, "What is the other person's point of view?"

But neither he nor Hahn ever understood the other's viewpoint.

Chapter 18
HOOBLER

Raymond L. Hoobler, a smart, tough, street-wise cop, thought he could buck the system. But when you run a police department by the book, reckless of the political consequences of refusing to bend to City Hall pressures, the future is predictable. The department had won its independence under Jansen, but political skills still were needed to work within the organization of city government. And public support was vital.

"He had earned his tough cop reputation in the hardest way, by being a tough cop, and for that reason he was doomed to a course that ultimately led to his resignation under fire," the 1981 police album asserted.

Hoobler's forte was the detective division. He was proud of his leadership on the street, both as a field lieutenant and later as an inspector. He was fully aware that they called him hard-line, hard-nose, ultra-conservative, and disciplinarian. He considered himself a realist who dealt with issues in a pragmatic way. But he proved to be something less than pragmatic in dealing with City Hall.

For more than two decades—during the terms of Jansen and Sharp—San Diego's police chiefs had had little interference from politicians and little trouble with city managers. But under Roed, the way of life of a chief again became one of conflict with City Hall and Hoobler was even more confrontational.

He had two big problems when he took over. One was rising crime, which had skyrocketed over a dozen years. The other was the sinking morale of his department. With a new chief, the force was off at a gallop in the 1970s, but to many the question was "To where?"

The cops and the dissidents were still fighting in San Diego streets. Criticism of police continued to be widespread among the general public, especially among young people, who saw the officers as the guardians of the established order. Hoobler, the street cop, tried to tell his troops the public was not judging individual officers. He also preached that they had to rise above the negativism of the press.

Hoobler was forty-three when he took the top cop job, a ruggedly handsome man of husky build, with dark wavy hair worn as short as a Marine recruit's. It took him twenty years of hard work to move up from the rank of $244-a-month patrolman to the pinnacle as a $1,840-a-month chief. Born August 23, 1927, in Bloomingdale, Ohio, he attended schools in Ohio and graduated from La Jolla High School in 1945.

He was working at the La Jolla post office at the time of his police appointment. He received an associate in science degree in police science from San Diego Community College in 1968, and taught there and on the faculties of the police academy and Grossmont Community College. He and his wife were parents of two daughters and a son.

Looking back, the 1981 San Diego police album gave this word picture: "With his crew cut and meticulously pressed uniform sporting four-star rank, he looked, walked, and talked like a cross between a Marine general and an old-fashioned conservative big-city police chief; neither of which images went well with a 'modern' city government."

In 1967, sixteen years after he joined the force on April 9, 1951, he was an inspector supervising the night patrol. He caught every riot and major disturbance in the city for sixteen months, gaining the confidence and admiration of officers for his ability as a stern-faced leader who could stand fast with them against barrages of rocks and sand-filled beer cans.

When a vacancy occurred on the chief's staff, Hoobler was one of four eligible inspectors, and he came out first on the promotion list. He told this story after retirement of how Chief Roed notified him: "I was in the hall outside the chief's office and through the open door he said, 'Oh, by the way, you're the new assistant chief; make arrangements to change offices.' That was my formal interview and unfortunately set the stage for my relationship with Roed."

Hoobler served only two months as an assistant chief. Within that two months the No. 2 chief, Jauregui, was demoted. Hoobler was on duty when summoned to City Manager Hahn's office at City Hall. There Chief Roed told Hoobler the manager wanted to make him the No. 2 man. "I had no advance knowledge of this appointment," Hoobler recalled.

"I don't think I contributed anything in my ten months as the No. 2 man," Hoobler said. "I didn't learn anything. It was just an exercise in frustration. I had very little, if anything, to say about the direction the department was taking."

Then came January 1971, and he was summoned from an up-state management school by City Manager Hahn, who said, "You are now the police chief."

Hoobler said that, when Hahn made him chief, Hahn also appointed Deputy Chief William D. Gore as the No. 2 commander. "There was no discussion about my choice," Hoobler said. "Hahn told me Bill Gore was going to be my No. 2 man. He didn't order, he just appointed Gore as my replacement. Hahn told me, 'You are forty-three years old and Gore is fifty-three, and he has had many more years of experience on the department. I think the two of you can complement each other.'" The news media had listed Gore, a veteran who was respected for his administrative ability, as the "front-runner" for the chief's job. Many officers thought Gore should have been given the top job.

The force was serving 735,000 citizens in the second largest city in California, covering an area of 386 square miles. This megalopolis included the harbor, beaches, reservoirs, military and industrial installations, both urban and rural areas, and twenty-two square miles comprising the southern police division along the international border.

Hoobler announced a departmental aim on March 29, 1971: "The goal is to contribute to the highest quality of life in maintaining a peaceful and orderly community." This "quality of life" statement came as a mild shock to old-time cops drilled in simpler ways of police thought.

Ray had definite ideas about the image he wanted his officers to present. "Roed eliminated the 'thunder-bucket' helmets in 1969, allowing the troops to go without headgear," Hoobler explained later. "Officers started letting their hair grow and they looked slovenly, like some of the people they dealt with. The evolution of long hair and fancy mustaches was the result of an attitude revolution. The POA was flexing its muscles. Everything in policing was changing.

"A couple of officers were wearing wigs on duty, and had their long hair up in curlers under the wigs. We had to discipline them because they couldn't wear gas masks effectively with a wig. I put the troops back in hard hats mainly because I think the public demanded the opportunity to identify an officer at the scene of an incident. The box hat says who is in charge."

This philosophy led to his transferring some detectives (many had been in street clothes for six years) to uniform patrol duty. That created near-mutiny. He put community relations officers in uniform although they had always worked in civilian clothing.

Chief Ray Hoobler. A smart, street-wise cop.

Was this the crux of all the discontent that developed? When asked this question, Hoobler in an interview after retirement replied: "But I wore a uniform. I was never ashamed of being identified as being a policeman."

Shortly after he took office, the city manager moved Hoobler into an office on the management floor at the City Administration Building many blocks from police headquarters. This also applied to other city department heads. Hahn wanted them all to be immediately available to him. Deputy Chief Gore from his office at headquarters ran the day-to-day operation. At first Hoobler thought this would be a benefit but soon changed his mind. He found he lacked the casual intelligence needed to lead the force. Behind Hoobler's back, many said Gore was the real chief and ran the department.

When Hahn retired, Hoobler returned to headquarters. Kimball Moore became the city manager on December 10, 1971, and by the spring of 1972 Moore and Hoobler were at loggerheads over the police budget, creating an "adversary relationship with the city manager's office that lasted as long as I was chief," Hoobler recalled.

There was an even more serious eroding factor—Hoobler's own attitude. He became more defiant and demanding. He alienated close associates and old friends on the force. He was criticized for being too outspoken when he thought candor was appropriate.

The kernel of the problem that developed with the City Council was his obsession with interpretation of the City Charter as it pertained to the police chief. "Nothing in this charter said the City Council should tell the police chief how to run his department," Hoobler said. He wanted to do it his way. "Some members of the council were very concerned about the Police Department. I refused to fix traffic tickets; refused to intercede in any drunk driving arrests. I knew my responsibility and was running the department."

This adversary relationship cost police many things, among them one that was priceless in creating citizen good will—operation of ambulances. When it decided to include paramedics in the ambulance program, the city took the service away from police and gave it to private paramedic/ambulance operators under contract with the city. Until then, police had operated seventeen station wagons converted to ambulances throughout the city.

The San Diego Narcotics Task Force, which Hoobler created in October 1973, is remembered as perhaps his greatest contribution to local law enforcement. City, state, and federal narcotic agencies had been operating independently without any coordination among them, several times endangering operations using regular and undercover officers. Originally the new task force consisted of three primary agencies—representatives of the Police Department, the Sheriff's Office, and the federal Drug Enforcement Agency. It was expanded to include other police departments in the county later, and other agencies had an open invitation to participate. Its objectives were to improve narcotic enforcement in the county by coordinating enforcement to avoid duplication of effort. The organization won national acclaim as a multi-agency force.

Early in his administration Hoobler, after a brush with federal and state affirmative action groups, decided to put policewomen in uniform and assign them to street duty. They had up to then been assigned only to investigative duties, wearing appropriate street clothing.

Of the fourteen policewomen, Hoobler allowed five who had been employed in 1954 (when the policewoman rating was restored by Jansen) to remain in investigative assignments. The rest were ordered into uniform, and some refused and resigned. The rest were reclassified as police officers, and five were assigned to the border inspection station at San Ysidro for a test period in 1971. None of the women in uniform went immediately on beat assignments. Connie Rae Van Putten (later to become the first woman lieutenant) and Alicia Daly Lampert were ultimately chosen to be the first to draw street duty, in full uniform, with gun belt and pistol, covering a beat in a cruiser.

The women on patrol were initiated into the raw life of the streets. Lampert recalled: "I stopped this woman driver for an illegal U-turn. I parked and walked up and looked into the driver's window and was startled. She had her blouse undone and her breasts hanging out. When she looked up and realized I was female, she really got ticked off. She knew and I knew what she was trying to do."

Van Putten recalled the night she was forced to fight a man to prove herself to male officers in the patio of the Market Street headquarters. She and a male partner had arrested a six-foot, 180-pound man who was drunk. He was in the back seat of their car when they drove into the patio. Connie put one handcuff on the man, and he shoved her backward. She claims her reaction was a lucky punch, but the prisoner went down, and when he came up his face was bleeding.

"I had a gut feeling one of the women officers on street duty was going to be seriously injured," Hoobler said later. "The male officers, primarily supervisors, fearing they would be criticized for being overly critical of the women, allowed second-level performance to slide by. As a result the department was overburdened with less than competent police personnel.

"There are many law enforcement jobs women can do very well, but being a field patrol officer is not one. There was no pressure to put the women on uniform patrol. I did it because I wanted to prove they were unsuited to street work. In the end it proved nothing."

It was a long row for the women police officers to hoe, but they progressed from being an oddity to being generally accepted by their male counterparts.

At the same time, two women in uniform were assigned to the school patrol section of the traffic bureau and took over training and supervising patrol functions at several elementary schools. This was a first because the patrol from its origination in 1936 had always been under the direction of male officers. Only boys had originally served on the patrol, but this also changed in mid-1971, when the program became coeducational and girls of the fifth and sixth grades became eligible for duty.

These were forward steps made by Hoobler, but the morale problem festered. The news media reported a growing number of resignations, low morale, and wholesale dissension. Friction developed between Hoobler and the city Civil Service Commission, to which officers appealed. In many cases, the commission held that the police chief was too harsh in his discipline. The attrition rate was high in Hoobler's first year: an average of seven officers a month left the department through resignation, termination, or retirement.

The inspection station at the San Ysidro border, which police had operated since 1958 with partial state funding, was closed July 17, 1975. Despite the impressive number of juveniles who had been diverted by police from visiting Tijuana unescorted, the recovery of stolen goods, and the many arrests made there during the seventeen years, the City Council closed the station when funding was withdrawn by the state. The main reason was doubt as to the legality of the border operation. Stopping juveniles who had committed no crime was a dubious proposition. Control of movements across the international border was considered to be exclusively the responsibility of the federal government. And sensitivity to legal limits on the scope of police work had been increasing steadily throughout the country.

One of the frustrating projects of the Hoobler administration was the nine months of monumental planning after San Diego was chosen for the August 1972 Republican National Convention. Then the Republicans shifted the event to Miami, Florida, citing trouble with preparation of the Sports Arena as the basis for the move.

Hoobler says he was subjected to more open council hearings than any police chief, before or after. A *Tribune* article by

Steven Casey on April 10, 1972, supported this claim, with a headline implying that council sessions were "charades, somewhere between a set-up and a circus. To call in Hoobler, sit him at a table, and force him to watch politicians grabbing for control of his department is to set him up like a clay pigeon and ask him to say he likes being shot at," Casey wrote. "To stage such a charade is to do him, his officers, and citizens a disservice. The council certainly has a legitimate voice in police practices affecting the public—but not the only voice, by a long shot."

The Police Department did not suffer from a fiscal standpoint. When Hoobler became chief in 1971, the budget was $15 million with 995 sworn officers. In his last year in 1975, the budget had jumped to $23 million with 1,200 sworn officers.

What pulled the rug out from under Hoobler was the charge that he violated the privacy of a psychological profile prepared by an officer assigned to counsel police personnel. Officer stresses included excessive drinking and marital problems. They had as many problems as ordinary civilians, perhaps more. Years before, one officer took to living in a tree. This officer worked in the City Jail where he solved sanitary problems and received meals as part of the job. He was using a tree for a home, Hoobler said, and the administration tried without success to get him a disability retirement on grounds of a mental breakdown.

Hoobler's problems escalated August 4, 1975, when the *Tribune* reported that the internal investigation unit, acting on the chief's orders, had seized confidential files on police personnel from the office of William J. Capps, a patrolman working full-time as a counselor. It was not the seizure itself which proved Hoobler's undoing, but his cover-up of his involvement in it.

Hoobler contended that the counseling was an "in-house" operation conducted by a sworn officer for police purposes and the files created were thus police property. After thirty-nine days of escalating controversy, complete with charges and countercharges reported by the news media, it all blew apart. Hoobler twice appeared before the City Council and denied he had authorized the seizure or known about it. He insisted the confidentiality of files had not been breached. But a full-scale investigation by City Manager Hugh McKinley showed Hoobler had told untruths on many counts and the manager apologized to the council for submitting "erroneous reports."

Hoobler, who until then had had an unblemished record of candor, honesty, and integrity, offered no defense at the time. In a 1983 interview, Hoobler said the news media "blew it all out of proportion." He thought he would have survived if he had gone before the council, but decided it was in the best interest of the force to quit. On September 7, 1975, he sent the city manager a letter stating "In view of the obvious increasing incompatibility between my office and the office of city manager, I have decided to resign my position effective September 9."

Close associates of Hoobler during this period, including his No. 2 man, Bill Kolender, had urged the chief to admit to the city manager that he had made a mistake, hoping to end the fiasco thus.

A *Tribune* editorial said: "[Hoobler's] lack of candor led directly to his resignation. He may have made mistakes but he never would have been required to resign because of these mistakes if he had been candid about the entire matter."

The man who prided himself on candor lacked it when he really needed it.

"Some hailed his departure as a great step forward for the department," the 1981 police album said. "Some of us, remembering his tactical skills, his straightforward manner of dealing with his subordinates and his unquestionable guts—well, we kind of wished he could have stepped into a closet until the heat dissipated and then have come back as our patrol captain."

Hoobler was forty-eight and by law could not draw a police pension, for which he was eligible, until age fifty. For seven months he did nothing, but then decided to go back to work. He became head of security for a Mission Valley hotel chain, and two years later was vice president in charge of corporate affairs. In the early 1980s he became a member of Sheriff John Duffy's Honorary Deputy Sheriffs Association, and served two years as its president.

He became the executive commissioner of the San Diego Crime Commission in 1987. This nonpartisan, nonprofit commission is funded by corporate and private contributions to work for the improvement of the justice system. In 1990, like several chiefs before him, he entered the race for county sheriff; and, like all the chiefs before him, he lost out. He then became a security consultant and managing partner of a Mission Hills travel service.

Hoobler has mellowed a little over the years and believes his opponents in the final controversy did him a favor. His health improved, and his second career has been rewarding and successful. "I miss my good friends, some still on the force, and miss the excitement of the job—but I certainly don't miss the political stress."

Would he do anything different if he had it to do over again? "Hell, no!"

The *Union* gave him credit for running a corruption-free organization and giving no special favors. His problems arose in public and political relations. His successor would demonstrate superlative savvy in just those fields.

Chapter 19
PRINCE OF THE CITY

A prophecy made by Elmer Jansen in the 1950s was about to come true.

Jansen's widow, Frances, said he told her in July 1956 of interviewing a young Jewish man for appointment to the force. "Elmer was quite impressed with the fellow, said he was handsome, intelligent, personable and made an excellent impression—and had been appointed," Mrs. Jansen recalled.

"Two years later Elmer came home and asked if I remembered the young Jewish officer he had hired. I did, because it was unusual for Jansen to be so enthused about anyone. Elmer pushed his hat back, leaned against the kitchen counter and quite deliberately said, 'Well, he is going to be chief of police some day.' "

This prediction came true seventeen years later when William Barnett Kolender, then forty, was appointed acting chief on September 9, 1975, the day Hoobler resigned. He was

Bill Kolender. A prediction he would be chief came true.

confirmed by the City Council on February 13, 1976, after the first public confirmation hearings in history. All elements of the community gave him their support.

Both Jansen and Kolender were well-liked by police officers. Jansen had strong city managers to work with, and when Kolender took the job he had a strong mayor, Pete Wilson. Both were able to work with the city councils and city managers they served. In Jansen's time the great majority of people had implicit faith in police; in Kolender's time things had changed radically, but he won the confidence of many who distrusted the police in general. Most important, both chiefs had political savvy.

Mayor Wilson's Crime Commission in a 1981 report gave this profile of what was wanted in police officers: "Courteous, polite and articulate, with quick responses, physical strength, and a good memory." That could be a general description of Kolender. He was born in Chicago, Illinois, on May 23, 1935, and came to San Diego at the age of eleven with his father, David S. Kolender, and mother, Esther. The father established a downtown jewelry store that he and his wife ran until shortly before his death in 1983.

Bill attended San Diego grammar schools and graduated in 1953 from Hoover High School. (The four police chiefs of the 1960s and 1970s, from Sharp to Kolender, were all graduates of local high schools.) When he was eighteen he joined the Navy and after honorable discharge he became a naval reserve. He was married and had a child a couple of months old by the time he was twenty-one. He was attending San Diego State University and working at a downtown surplus store to make ends meet when he walked a beat a couple of times with a friend who was a cop.

"I decided to join the force," Kolender said, "not particularly to become a cop, but mainly because I needed something to support us while I went to school. I got to like it, and it liked me, and I stayed. I'm not sorry at all. I love it."

When he joined, not many officers had attended college, and few held degrees. He had a bachelor's degree with a major in public administration. By 1984, everyone on his staff held a college degree.

All types of vehicles for any terrain were being used by San Diego police late in the 1980s. Left: the "TAC" (Tactical Motorcycle Unit), a highly visible patrol squad used citywide, equipped with lightweight, off-road cycles. Right: A more leisurely, but useful, patrol by bicycle is used in beach areas.

In 1984, Kolender compared the Jansen era with his:

> Jansen brought the force into the twentieth century. He took a mediocre, basically corrupt organization and made it into a professional police department, respected throughout the state and nation for competency. He set a tone of integrity for this department that is still dominant.
>
> When I took over, three things had to be done. One was to build a relationship of trust, communication and integrity between the police administration and city government. Even though we are a part of the same government, the perception was "we/they" and they were out to get us. You must realize that City Hall is the only ballgame in town and in order to get more equipment, more salaries, what you need to move the department, you've got to play ball with the guy that's got the baseball.
>
> Secondly, because of all the adverse publicity, the public didn't have a very good image of police. So you had to build it with the public.
>
> Third and probably the most important, the cops were really ticked off at the administration, as evidenced by the No. 1 factor—the Police Officers Association hired the Teamsters union to represent them as a body.
>
> All three things had to change.

The San Diego Police Officers Association in June 1975 had signed a $190,000 representation contract with the Teamsters union. The 1,100 officers sought a 5 percent pay hike. Kolender on November 6 said in a speech at the convention of the Police Officers Research Association of California (a statewide lobbying arm of law enforcement): "If we unionize police, professionalization is gone. If we are going to be a profession, we are going to have our own union." Kolender could speak with assurance, since he had been elected twice by his fellow officers as president of the Police Officers Association. In a year and a half the Teamsters were no longer representing the police.

That instantly improved the relationship between the police and City Hall, but Kolender set out to make more improvements. He hosted the city manager and members of the City Council at a day-long meeting at police headquarters in February 1978, giving them a tour of the station. After lunch, the chief and his top assistants briefed city leaders. This was the first time an entire council met at headquarters.

To rebuild police-citizen relations was a more difficult task. The horse patrol, the bicycle patrol, and the walking beat were long gone, and with them the close relationship between the officers and the public. A citizen seldom encountered an officer except to get a traffic ticket. Bill Kolender—with his interest, training, and experience in human relations—realized that people had changed. They were products of a society that in the 1960s had turned many against the police.

Throughout his administration, he sought to put officers on the spot where they could be seen and appreciated while doing their job to protect and to serve. A better relationship with City Hall made it possible to form and equip special patrol units such as the following:

• A tactical team on small motorcycles for faster response in congested areas.

Left: Sgt. Manny Lopez, one of the commanders of the special border detail to protect illegal immigrants from robbery, assault or rape. Right: Five San Diego chiefs of police in 1977. Seated, left to right, A.E. Jansen, W.S. Sharp, and Jimmy Roed. Standing, Bill Kolender and Ray Hoobler.

• Use of bicycles in an expanded beach patrol.

• Revival of the horse patrols in downtown and Balboa Park areas, and for special events.

• A canine patrol, with seven dogs and police-handlers, one for each of the seven divisional stations.

• A new policy on number of officers per police car. Kolender became convinced that the number of officers per car should be based on need: one officer was enough in some areas, two were needed in others. In the 1984 budget he was given twenty more officers to create special two-man patrols.

• Expanded use of walking officers in the Gaslamp Quarter downtown, along El Cajon Boulevard, and wherever street prostitution or drug dealing became obnoxious.

Kolender himself became a symbol of a closer police-community relationship. He was active in many community affairs. He was seen in news photos as often in a dinner jacket as in a uniform. He was a prince of the city.

And Kolender was active in professional organizations on the state and national levels. Gov. Edmund G. Brown, Jr., appointed him to the state commission on Peace Officers Standards and Training (POST). Kolender was named to a new state narcotics commission. He became chairman of the Major Cities Organization of the Chiefs of Police and a member of the executive commission of the International Association of Chiefs of Police. Gov. George Deukmejian appointed Kolender to the state Board of Governors of the California Community Colleges, important to the police since so many officers were being trained in community colleges.

Police morale was improved by relaxation of grooming and dress restrictions, with long hair permitted as long as it was neat. The chief revived a monthly house organ and started a biweekly videotape chat in which he answered questions by officers.

Kolender had a seasoned group of deputy chiefs on his staff. In mid-1977 his first assistant chief, Jim Connole, retired, and Kolender appointed Robert W. (Bob) Burgreen as the No. 2 man. (The terminology of high rank on the chief's staff has changed often in recent years. The titles of deputy chief and assistant chief became interchangeable, according to the preference of the chief in office. But there was never any doubt as to who was No. 2.)

Kolender also appointed Manuel E. Guaderrama to deputy chief on July 28, 1983, giving him the highest rank attained by a Hispanic in the department. (The previously highest-ranking was Detective Lieutenant Joe Lopez, who was born in 1877 in an adobe house in Old Town and was a highly respected officer from 1910 until his retirement in 1936.)

Kolender created a border task force of ten officers under the direction of Lieutenant Dick Snider and Sergeant Manny Lopez, to protect illegal aliens from attack, robbery, and rape along the city's eight miles of international border with Mexico. He established BARF (Border Alien Robbery Force) in 1976 and disbanded it in 1978. During the 1976–78 operation there were seven shoot-outs, with three BARF members wounded and the unit killing or wounding seven Mexicans. The extreme violence of the operation resulted in its being suspended, but it was reinstated in January 1984, working with U. S. border patrolmen.

Other special units were created. A gang detail was developed to combat rising gang problems such as drive-by shootings. A Metro Arson Strike Team (MAST) was formed in conjunction with the Fire Department. Special beach enforcement teams, one a boat patrol unit, focused on seasonal problems. A narcotics street team targeted low-level street dealers. Chief Kolender used more civilians in positions not requiring enforcement powers, increasing the number of sworn officers available for patrol duties. By the summer of 1988, a total of sixty community service officers were assisting regular police in the Neighborhood Watch program, in crime prevention in Balboa Park, and in staffing nine police storefronts around the city.

All of this took money. In 1984 Kolender commented thus on police funding: "Our 1968 budget was $8 million dollars. Today it is a little less than $80 million. We used to get more cops and didn't get cars for them. Now we have a formula. We get more cops, we get more supervisors, we get more desks, cars and more radios. We get everything or we don't get cops."

Before the end of his second year in office, Kolender announced that the department would be decentralized, with stations to be opened in five other areas of the city, in addition to the existing northern Division in the Golden Triangle area of northeast La Jolla and the Southern Division in San Ysidro.

Studies had concluded that the crowded old headquarters on Market Street reduced efficiency. With only two substations, a change of shift meant some officers had to drive as far as twenty miles to reach their beats.

By 1980 decentralization was in high gear, with five new commands, each under a captain in temporary buildings. In mid-1984 the first permanent building, for the Western Division on Gaines Street in Mission Valley, was dedicated. It was built at a cost of $1.9 million.

Other substations were built for the Eastern Division on Aero Drive across from Montgomery Field on Kearny Mesa;

Above: The ten-man BARF detail (Border Alien Robbery Force) on night patrol in the dangerous Tijuana river bottom on the International Border. Below: Two officers of the police gang detail search a suspect against a graffiti-marked wall, bearing special symbols of different gangs.

Northeastern in Peñasquitos; and Southeastern on Skyline Drive. Also, provision was made for a new Central Division downtown.

The biggest project was the replacement of the 1939 headquarters building at 801 West Market Street, built on port tidelands during the Depression, primarily with federal funds. The Spanish-style quadrangle was charming but was intended for a force sixteen times smaller than the one in existence.

Commander Ken Fortier, who had been responsible for installation of a computer-assisted dispatch system, was named by Kolender to head a division to oversee the building program. Fortier had read an article in a bond magazine on the use of "Certificates Of Participation" in financing public buildings. COP is a form of long-term lease-purchase financing in which investors receive proportion-ate shares of the lease payments on municipal projects. Fortier sold Kolender, City Manager Ray Blair, and the City Council on the idea, and the first COP was used to build the Western Division station.

A long-time dream of a new, high-tech and fully equipped headquarters became a reality when officers moved into this seven-story structure at 1401 Broadway in November 1986. A modern crime laboratory, communications system, and tight security system were featured.

This worked so well that Fortier also gained approval to use COPs for financing a new headquarters. A block bounded by Broadway, Fourteenth, Fifteenth, and E was chosen as the site. A 165,000-square-foot building, seven stories high with levels beneath for parking 820 vehicles, was designed and financed with $43.7 million in COPs. Payments to investors, including interest, will total $141.5 million over thirty years. But the city expects to pay off the certificates earlier. The headquarters and a $4.8-million main police garage nearby were constructed by the M. H. Golden Company for the Starboard Development Company. The financing arrange-ment was not greatly different from the lease negotiated early in the century for a new police station and jail on Second Street. The cost of that earlier project was only about $200,000.

Ground was broken for the new building at 1401 Broadway on January 30, 1985. On January 16, 1987, the flag was lowered for the last time at the Market Street station; the building was abandoned and turned back to the Port District.

(The first official moving day was November 11, 1986, and was followed by similar mov-ing days each weekend until the old quarters were vacant.) Actual occupancy of the new building had been delayed by late delivery of $1.7 million worth of new furniture. Grand opening ceremonies were held January 30, 1987.

Police moved into a high-tech edifice with two entrances, one a large public plaza on Broadway leading into a secure lobby, part of a tight security system. The other entrance, on E Street, provided access to public parking and to the Central Division, located on this level. Featured in the new headquarters was an ultra-modern laboratory and foren-sic facility. Eventually the communications division, located in the City Operations Building base-ment, was moved to the headquarters, when $1.7 mil-lion in equipment and instal-lation costs were funded. The gray-and-blue glass exterior handsomely sheathes a police headquarters that from a dis-tance appears to be a high-rise business building. The palm and ficus trees at the plaza entrance give the layout the appearance of a modern hotel.

These were the visible signs that the city was booming and the police force was booming along with it. But the biggest headlines were written by the kind of unpredictable tragedy that policemen have always faced in their daily work.

There was nothing about that Monday morning, September 25, 1978, to portend disaster. The blue sky was washed clean by a seasonal Santa Ana condition. Flight 182 of Pacific Southwest Airlines, a Boeing 727-200 jet, inbound from Sacramento and Los Angeles, passed over Mission Valley, coming in for a landing at Lindbergh Field. The PSA pilot had been warned by air controllers of a single-engine Cessna a mile away. A minute and five seconds after this warning, the two planes collided in midair over North Park, plunging the small Cessna with its instructor and student pilot to their deaths on Polk Avenue.

The airliner went down in flames in an explosive crash at Dwight and Nile streets, snuffing out 135 lives in the jet and 7 more on the ground, with a total death toll of 144. This was one of the greatest disasters in the history of the city and at the time was the nation's highest death toll in a single airliner crash.

A woman police radio dispatcher, Billie Crow, veteran of many disaster drills, in all the confusion maintained some semblance of order until a command post was set up nearby. At the height of the disaster operation, 674 policemen were involved. Mayor Pete Wilson, Chief Kolender, and Fire Chief Dee Rogers had high praise for all their officers.

There remained mental scars—images of the crash scene lingered in officers' minds. A year before the disaster Kolender had approved psychiatric help for officers with job-related problems. After the PSA crash, policemen sought counseling offered by the Academy of San Diego Psychologists. By 1980 Kolender had fully implemented the department's Employee Assistance Program with Dr. Michael Mantell, a psychiatrist, in charge.

SWAT team member ready for action.

represent law and order and to take their lives is reprehensible."

When Patrolman James P. Lewis was shot and killed on December 28, 1970, he was the first San Diego policeman killed by gunfire in thirty-six years and eleven months. But in the period from 1977 to 1988, eleven officers died in the line of duty, ten from gunshots and one fatally injured by a hit-run driver.

Responding to a request by the Police Officers Association, after the fatal shooting of three policemen and the wounding of two others, Kolender launched a study of officer safety. It probed all aspects of departmental policies and procedures. When the study group, headed by Deputy Chief Norm Stamper, urged that bullet-proof vests be made mandatory for patrol duty, Kolender agreed and put the new policy into effect in the fall of 1985. Ninety-six recommendations were made during the study. (Not all changes in safety procedures were made public.)

Meanwhile, a rising tide of violence in the mid-1970s had become one of the major problems for the department. Violence was directed not only against civilians but against officers, and by the 1980s it had taken a shocking toll of policemen gunned down on duty. There was a significant increase in narcotics-, gang-, and prostitution-related crimes. The swollen population, changing social attitudes, urbanization, and uncertain economic situations also contributed. The percentage of "personalized" homicides (people killed by those they knew) decreased as the violence became more senseless and more vicious. Children were shot down in cold blood along with adults. Kolender said that in some parts of the city practically every car stopped by police contained a gun. He repeatedly warned: "If you pull a gun on a San Diego police officer you are punching your ticket—you are contemplating suicide. I do not expect these officers to be shot before they shoot."

Never in history had the homicide toll included so many policemen. "I am devastated by these murders of police officers," Kolender said in 1984. "These men and women

No one, no matter how hardened to the new violence in the streets, could predict the nightmare in San Ysidro on the afternoon of July 16, 1984—a massacre in a McDonald's restaurant where twenty-two people, including a deranged heavily armed gunman, died in the nation's worst single shooting incident to that date. The massacre began about 4 o'clock and continued sporadically until the gunman, James Oliver Huberty, was killed by a SWAT officer's bullet at 5:15 p.m. In the initial outburst of shotgun and automatic rifle fire, Huberty shot to death or fatally wounded twenty-one men, women, and children and wounded nineteen others. Of the twenty-one slain, nine were between eight months and eighteen years of age.

Kolender celebrated his tenth anniversary as top cop the next year on a wave of popularity. He had ushered in a new era on becoming acting chief in September 1975. He served during the decade under his mentor, City Manager Ray Blair, and soon was to serve under a second manager, Sylvester Murray, upon Blair's retirement. Kolender had declined overtures to run for mayor in the elections of 1983 and 1985,

The city was staggered by the heavy toll of slain policemen in the mid-1980s. The Union said, "No one says goodbye like the police, especially when the officer has met a violent death." These pictures were taken at the funeral of rookie Jerry Hartless.

Opposite page left: Sagon A. Penn. Right: WE CAN (Walking Enforcement Campaign Against Narcotics) on patrol in Southeast San Diego as street-dealing suspects are questioned and searched by Patrolman Kevin Ammon and Police Officer Maura McKenas-Parga.

turned down an offer to be chief of the San Diego Fire Department, and rejected a formal offer to become head of the U. S. Immigration and Naturalization Service.

But then the loving honeymoon, the carefully orchestrated improvement in community relations ended, and Kolender found himself in deep trouble.

A traffic stop turned sour in Encanto in the southeastern area of the city on the night of March 31, 1985, leaving one police officer dead, another shot, and a woman ride-along passenger wounded. The shootings would become an albatross around the department's neck, polarizing racial relations in San Diego during the two years of drama that unfolded in two trials of a twenty-three-year-old black man, Sagon A. Penn, who was accused of the shootings.

Penn, a karate expert, was tried for the shooting and wounding of Police Agent Donovan Joseph Jacobs, twenty-eight; the shooting and killing of Jacobs's fellow agent, Thomas Edward Riggs, twenty-seven, a five-year veteran; and the shooting and wounding of Sarah Piña-Ruiz, thirty-two, a mother of two who was riding with Riggs as a civilian observer.

The bloodshed occurred in the 6500 block of Brooklyn Avenue after Jacobs, searching for an armed gang member, stopped a truck driven by Penn and carrying eight other people. Several prosecution witnesses testified under oath that Jacobs, after asking for Penn's driver's license and being given a wallet instead of the license removed from the wallet, instigated a scuffle with Penn, directed racial slurs toward him, and hit him repeatedly with a baton. Testimony in other instances apparently contradicted statements given by the same witnesses to police during the hours immediately following the shootings.

After a week-long preliminary hearing, Municipal Judge J. Richard Haden dismissed assertions that Penn had been stopped unlawfully and was acting in self-defense when he grabbed the holstered revolver of Jacobs and began firing. The judge held that the officers struck Penn with fists and batons as he resisted their lawful efforts to arrest him.

Penn was tried for killing Riggs, shooting Jacobs in the neck, and then walking to Riggs's patrol car, where Piña-Ruiz sat, and after saying, "You are a witness," shooting and wounding her superficially in the side, back, and arm. Penn left the scene in Jacobs's patrol car after running over Jacobs as the wounded Piña-Ruiz (in Riggs's car) radioed for help. Penn drove to his grandfather's home, where he asked what to do, claiming he shot in self-defense. As advised, he then surrendered at police headquarters.

Penn was acquitted of seven charges in the first trial, including the murder of Officer Riggs and attempted murder of Officer Jacobs. On other charges the jury deadlocked. The district attorney's office asked for a retrial and added two counts of assault. At the end of the second trial, the jury deadlocked on the two assault charges and the lesser offense of involuntary manslaughter in the death of officer Riggs. The next day the district attorney dropped the remaining charges, saying in a written statement: "I think it is time this community put this case behind us."

Penn at the end was a free man after his defense attorney twice successfully argued that the accused was the victim of a brutal, racist attack, and that he seized and fired the officer's gun only in self-defense against excessive force.

The acquittal of Sagon Penn severely shook the department but pleased many in the black community and set off complaints of police harassment of minorities and cries of "Fire the chief!"

In July 1987, the trial judge delivered a scathing rebuke of police conduct during Penn's second trial. Superior Court Judge J. Morgan Lester publicly accused the officers of being

Left: Sgt. Cheryl Meyers was working a special detail late in the 1980s when she made this arrest in Balboa Park. The park had become more dangerous and security tightened after the murder of an actor there. Right: Another problem which required more police attention in the same period was street people who frequented the downtown area. The department resorted to foot patrols. Patrolman R. Graham holds a curbside conference.

involved in "nightstick justice" during their confrontation with Penn. Judge Lester also accused officers of lying on the witness stand to protect other officers, and said the department tried to conceal or alter evidence. This led to a request by Kolender and District Attorney Ed Miller for an investigation by the state attorney general.

Attorney General John Van de Kamp announced in April 1988 that his investigators had identified nine instances of wrongdoing but did not find evidence to warrant prosecution. This decision was reached when it was determined that Penn would not be a credible witness.

This was followed by an editorial in the *Union* under the headline, "It's Time to Lay the Penn Case to Rest," with Kolender's comment: "Enough suffering has been done." The *Union* concluded the Penn case had tormented San Diego long enough, and for once and all, this painful chapter in the city's history should end. But it just wouldn't die, critically altering countless lives. There was no happy ending, no easy answer.

Kolender would bounce from crisis to crisis for several years, stalked by controversy and embarrassments, but through it all he kept his cool and his badge. The chief believed the two years of media coverage of the murder trials caused undeserved negative public reaction to the force. His previous excellent relations with the news media were strained several times. The media became more skeptical of police and their tactics. His relations with minority communities also suffered.

A barrage of charges of heavy-handed tactics continued, which resulted in the city forming its first citizens advisory board to investigate allegations of police misconduct. Controversy followed because members of the board were appointed by Chief Kolender and John Lockwood, who had succeeded Sylvester Murray as city manager.

A new police training program in human relations and defense tactics was instituted after the Penn shootings, at a time when the city led the nation in the death rate of on-duty officers. The first black police administrator, Leroy T. Brady, thirty-nine, a management consultant, was appointed director of department personnel services.

These were progressive steps by Kolender, but in November 1986 the chief received a written reprimand (his first ever) after an investigation by the city manager confirmed newspaper reports that Kolender was involved in ticket fixing for relatives and friends and in other administrative improprieties, including using a uniformed officer to run personal errands on a daily basis. Assistant Chief Burgreen also received a reprimand. Then several officers complained that they had been treated unfairly in disability cases. This caused friction between the Police Department and the city Civil Service Commission.

Through it all, Kolender kept his humor. In 1987, while being feted by fellow officers for thirty-one years of service in law enforcement, he said, "The first thirty years felt like one; the last year felt like thirty." He admitted his faults and went about his business, maintaining that he addressed each crisis as it arose in "an undefensive, honest and open manner."

By 1988, the increase in drug traffic and gang violence had brought minority residents closer to their Police

Left: With a green sash across his chest, Chief Bill Kolender leads the color guard in a Saint Patrick's Day parade. Above: Chief Robert W. Burgreen, thirtieth to hold the position, led the force into the second century of its existence. Burgreen, forty-nine when promoted, had been assistant chief to Kolender for eleven years. Native of Carlsbad, coastal city north of San Diego, he had been a county resident all his life. He was the sixth chief appointed from the ranks since 1947.

Department. They held community meetings, inviting police to attend and contribute, and the police responded. When thirteen drive-by shootings were recorded over six days in the spring of 1988, officers from the Special Response Team were put into the field, working primarily in the city's Southeastern, Eastern, and Central districts. Two weeks later this task force added a SWAT member armed with a submachine gun to each special patrol unit. This was the first time officers in patrol cars, even on special duty, had carried the high-powered weapons.

Longtime Kolender colleague John Lockwood, who rose through the ranks of city government to the top position as city manager in 1986, remained steadfast in his support and in his belief the chief had the ability to get things done.

Kolender repeatedly said he planned to serve until July 1990 unless offered "something too good to turn down." On June 23, 1988, he announced he would take retirement on July 1. At age fifty-three, after thirteen years as chief and thirty-two years on the force, he was leaving the job of chief, paying $83,000 yearly, to become assistant to the publisher of the Union-Tribune Publishing Company. His new job would focus on community relations and educational programs; he would not be involved in the news or editorial policies of the two newspapers, the *Union* and the *Tribune*. He said his decision to take the new job had nothing to do with any of his past problems as chief. He believed he was leaving a strong staff behind under Acting Chief Robert W. Burgreen.

After a period of recruitment, City Manager Lockwood nominated Burgreen, forty-nine, to lead the department into its second century of protecting and serving San Diegans. The assistant chief for eleven years during the Kolender administration, Burgreen as the thirtieth chief of police had a top priority of restoring the credibility of the department. When he took over he had served twenty-eight years on the force. His promotion carried a pay raise of $4,000 to an annual salary of about $84,000. Burgreen chose Deputy Chief Norman Stamper as his No. 2 man.

It seemed to many on the department that an era of stability was assured under Chief Burgreen. Before his administration, six chiefs of police had served in forty-eight years, from Cliff Peterson—who took office in March 1940—to Jansen, Sharp, Roed, Hoobler, and Kolender. This contrasts sharply with the ten chiefs in ten years during the 1930s. Of the last seven chiefs, including Burgreen, all came from the ranks.

Kolender fell short by a year of equaling the record of Elmer Jansen, chief for fourteen years. One thing was sure, that Kolender would be missed, for where else in these United States could you find a Jewish chief of police leading a bunch of Irish cops in a Saint Patrick's Day parade? Only in America's finest city.

ROLL OF HONOR

1913–1991

GUNSHOT, No. 1—CAMPBELL, Emery E., 33, patrolman, died of gunshot wound, answering call of man with gun at Fifth Avenue and G Street, scene of shooting, August 27, 1913.

TRAFFIC/MANSLAUGHTER, No. 2—HOPKINS, Oliver S., 47, motorcycle officer, deliberately run over and killed by truck on M (Imperial) Street between 19th and 20th Streets, July 2, 1915.

MISCELLANEOUS, No. 3—HOLCOMB, Walter B., 33, patrolman, died from Spanish influenza contracted during epidemic of 1918 while transporting dying flu victim from train station to hospital, October 21, 1918.

TRAFFIC ACCIDENT, No. 4—LEE, Joseph S., 33, motorcycle officer, killed chasing a speeder, collided with oil truck at India and Cedar streets, March 19, 1921.

GUNSHOT, No. 5—HARRIS, Charles R., 51, detective, shot to death while on a stakeout with policewoman in police undercover car for a petting party bandit in grove of trees in Balboa Park back of Roosevelt School, April 3, 1927.

TRAFFIC ACCIDENT, No. 6—POWERS, Robert L., 30, motorcycle officer, killed chasing a speeder on Barnett Avenue near the old Ryan Air Field, crashed head-on with an auto, June 16, 1928.

MISCELLANEOUS (fatally clubbed), No. 7—McPHERSON, Robert B., patrolman, fatally clubbed in city jail by prisoner while on jail duty, Sept. 19, 1929, died September 20, 1929.

GUNSHOT, NO. 8—MOORE, Edward J., 31, patrolman, shot January 7, 1933, at 13th and G streets when he sought to question his assailant. Died January 15, 1933.

MISCELLANEOUS (exhaustion), No. 9—KEAYS, Thomas A., 52, patrolman, died of exhaustion in Second Avenue police station after helping remove mangled body from beneath trolley car at Second Avenue and Broadway, November 20, 1937. Oldest officer to die in the course of duty.

TRAFFIC ACCIDENT, No. 10—GOODRICH, Henry J., 38, motorcycle officer, killed when his cycle and an auto collided at the top of Torrey Pines grade on Highway 101 while on patrol, September 7, 1940.

TRAFFIC ACCIDENT, No. 11—BOWERS, Robert F., 33, patrolman, died in collision of patrol car and a truck at Texas Street and Polk Avenue during pursuit of a speeder on December 12, 1955.

TRAFFIC ACCIDENT, No. 12—KAY, Harry, Jr., 33, sergeant, killed while chasing a speeder in his patrol car in Rose Canyon near the old brickyard on old Highway 101 when involved in a multi-vehicle collision on March 11, 1957.

TRAFFIC ACCIDENT, No. 13—BUSHMAN, Michael J., patrolman, killed when thrown out of patrol car when it overturned on Paradise Valley Road east of Munda Road, November 25, 1963.

TRAFFIC ACCIDENT, No. 14—EVERITT, Robert A., 37, sergeant, killed when struck by a pickup truck while directing traffic at previous accident scene in eastbound lanes of Highway 80 (now I-8) a quarter of a mile east of Taylor Street on December 7, 1964.

GUNSHOT, No. 15—LEWIS, James P., 23, patrolman, fatally shot at 3048 Midway Drive in parking lot of a bar while attempting to check identification of two men denied admission to bar. Shot near midnight December 12, 1970, died December 29, 1970. Youngest officer to die on duty. First gunshot death of a San Diego police officer in 36 years and 11 months.

GUNSHOT, No. 16—EDWARDS, Freddie J., 34, sergeant, shot to death investigating a robbery of a 7-11 market at 5202 El Cajon Blvd., October 7, 1971.

GUNSHOT, No. 17—ALLEN, Denis W., 34, patrolman, shot to death in gunfight in a Golden Hills apartment at 2720 Broadway after answering a call about a man with a knife. Assailant also killed. April 2, 1977.

GUNSHOT, No. 18—BUGGS, Archie C., 30, patrolman, shot to death on November 4, 1977, after making a routine traffic stop and while writing citation in the 7100 block of Skyline Drive. First black officer to die in the line of duty.

GUNSHOT, No. 19—ANAYA, Michael T., 25, patrolman, fatally shot while answering a disturbance call in the 4100 block of Altadena Avenue on March 21, 1979. Died April 11, 1979. Assailant, who shot Anaya with officer's service revolver, shot and killed himself.

TRAFFIC ACCIDENT, No. 20—GONZALES, Dennis G., 25, patrolman, killed outright June 25, 1979, when struck by a hit-and-run driver while making a traffic stop on eastbound side of Interstate 8 freeway, east of Fairmount Avenue. Driver responsible later surrendered.

GUNSHOT, No. 21—TIFFANY, Harry K., 32, patrolman, killed June 6, 1981, while answering disturbance call at 2436 Crandall Drive, Linda Vista. Assailant killed by SWAT team. First time in history of department two officers killed in same incident.

GUNSHOT, No. 22—EBELTOFF, Ronald R., 34, patrolman, died June 6, 1981, of gunshot wounds received in the Linda Vista incident that resulted in death No. 21.

GUNSHOT, No. 23—JOHNSON, Kirk L., 26, patrolman, fatally shot February 20, 1983, when he drove his patrol car without lights into a parking lot off Genesee Avenue south of State Route 52 to investigate suspicious car. Found by fellow officers dying behind wheel of his car, engine running and in gear, foot on brake pedal.

GUNSHOT, No. 24—TONAHILL, Kimberly Sue, 24, rookie policewoman, fatally shot September 14, 1984, while making routine stop and issuing citation in wooded area known as Grape Street Park in Balboa Park. First woman officer slain on duty since policewomen put on streets ten years before. This also was a slaying of two officers in same incident, with a third officer also wounded; worst street incident in department history. Assailant later found hiding in park.

GUNSHOT, No. 25—RUOPP, Timothy J., 31, patrolman, fatally wounded in same incident as death No. 24. Shot September 14, 1984, died September 16, 1984. Third officer, Gary Mitrovich, 26, patrolman, shot in shoulder, recovered.

GUNSHOT, No. 26—RIGGS, Thomas E., 27, patrolman with rating as agent, brother-in-law of victim No. 25 and son of retired SDPD Sergeant Charles Riggs. Shot to death during routine stop on Brooklyn Avenue in Encanto March 31, 1985. Second patrolman, Agent Donovan Jacobs, and a woman ride-along were wounded in this incident and both recovered. Suspect, Sagon A. Penn, 23, escaped from scene, later surrendered, admitting the shootings. After two lengthy trials, the last ending in 1987, Penn walked free after acquittals and the district attorney's decision to drop the remaining charges.

GUNSHOT, No. 27—HARTLESS, Jerry L., 24, rookie patrolman, shot night of January 9, 1988, at eastern end of Manomet Street in Southeast San Diego, died January 31, 1988. Fatally wounded while chasing a man suspected of selling drugs.

GUNSHOT, No. 28—DAVIS, Ronald W., 24, two-year veteran, killed an hour before dawn on September 17, 1991, answering family disturbance call at Paradise Hills apartment, Meadowbrook Drive near Paradise Valley Road. Died 6:20 a.m. in Mercy Hospital of wounds to neck and arm. Gunned down without a chance in a parking lot. Assailant Arnoldo De Villa Castillo, 34, resident of the apartment complex, escaped in darkness and fog, setting off massive manhunt. Castillo, spotted at 4:30 p.m. same day hiding in bushes surrounding complex, refused to drop .45 automatic he held. Officers opened fire. Autopsy revealed Castillo a suicide with bullet in forehead. Davis survived by wife, Wendy, and two sons, age 4 and 18 months.

TOTAL, 28. GUNSHOT, 16. TRAFFIC, 8. MISCELLANEOUS, 3. TRAFFIC/MANSLAUGHTER, 1. YOUNGEST, 23 years old, OLDEST 52.

LIST OF CHIEFS

CHIEF

		From	To
1	COYNE, Joseph	05-16-89	05-26-91
2	CRAWFORD, William H.	05-27-91	07-27-91
3	PRINGLE, W. H.	07-28-91	08-27-91
4	BRENNING, Jacob	08-28-91	05-09-97
5	RUSSELL, James	05-10-97	05-04-99
6	BUSHYHEAD, Edward W.	05-05-99	05-31-03
7	THOMAS, Albert A.	06-01-03	06-16-07
8	MOULTON, George W.	06-17-07	09-03-07
9	NEELY, William T.	09-04-07	04-30-09
10	WILSON, Jefferson "Keno"	05-03-09	01-10-17
11	STEER, Joseph E.	01-11-17	05-04-17
	PATRICK, James (acting)	05-05-17	10-09-17
12	McMULLEN, Steward P.	10-10-17	04-08-19
13	PATRICK, James	04-09-19	05-31-27
14	DORAN, Joseph W.	06-01-27	05-12-29
15	HILL, Arthur R.	05-13-29	05-03-31
16	BENBOUGH, Percival James	05-04-31	08-03-31
17	SCOTT, Harry H.	08-26-31	06-11-32
18	PETERSON, John T.	06-12-32	07-31-32
19	NEWSOM, Robert P.	08-01-32	06-04-33
20	RAYMOND, Harry J.	06-05-33	09-01-33
21	PETERSON, John T.	09-02-33	09-06-34
22	SEARS, George Meredith	09-07-34	04-27-39
	KELLY, Harry J. (acting)	04-28-39	07-18-39
23	PETERSON, John T.	07-19-39	03-20-40
24	PETERSON, Clifford E.	03-21-40	10-15-47
25	JANSEN, Adam Elmer	10-16-47	01-07-62
26	SHARP, Wesley S.	01-08-62	01-03-68
27	ROED, Olif "Jimmy"	01-04-68	03-11-71
28	HOOBLER, Ray L.	03-11-71	09-09-75
	KOLENDER, William B.(acting)	09-10-75	02-13-76
29	KOLENDER, William B.	02-13-76	07-29-88
	BURGREEN, Robert W. (acting)	07-30-88	09-18-88
30	BURGREEN, Robert W.	09-19-88	

CODE OF ETHICS

★

As a Law Enforcement Officer, my fundamental duty is to serve mankind; to safeguard lives and property; to protect the innocent against deception, the weak against oppression or intimidation, and the peaceful against violence or disorder; and to respect the constitutional rights of all men to liberty, equality and justice.

I will keep my private life unsullied as an example to all; maintain courageous calm in the face of danger, scorn, or ridicule; develop self-restraint; and be constantly mindful of the welfare of others. Honest in thought and deed in both my personal and official life, I will be exemplary in obeying the laws of the land and the regulations of my department. Whatever I see or hear of a confidential nature or that is confided to me in my official capacity will be kept ever secret unless revelation is necessary in the performance of my duty.

I will never act officiously or permit personal feelings, prejudices, animosities or friendships to influence my decisions. With no compromise for crime and with relentless prosecution of criminals, I will enforce the law courteously and appropriately without fear or favor, malice or ill will, never employing unnecessary force or violence and never accepting gratuities.

I recognize the badge of my office as a symbol of public faith, and I accept it as a public trust to be held so long as I am true to the ethics of the police service. I will constantly strive to achieve these objectives and ideals, dedicating myself before God to my chosen profession, law enforcement.

[This document originated with officers of the San Diego Police Department and has been adopted by many other departments in California and throughout the United States]

Broadway in 1929, looking west from Seventh Street.

SOURCES

★

Annual reports, chiefs of police to mayor and council, City of San Diego, 1890–1985, archives of the City of San Diego.

Bellon, Walter, "Memoirs," unpublished, 1935, Research Archives, San Diego Historical Society.

Castanien, Pliny R., papers relating to the San Diego police, 1948–1989, collected by the author, Research Archives, San Diego Historical Society.

Commemorative Police Albums: 1914, 1922, 1924, 1925, 1927, 1981, 1986.

Diehl, Robert, "To Speak or Not Speak," unpublished master's thesis, University of San Diego, 1976.

Fall In and Informant, published monthly, 1950–1989, San Diego Police Officers Association.

Flash and Up Front, published monthly, San Diego Police Department, 1941–1989.

Heilbron, Carl H., History of San Diego County, San Diego Press Club, San Diego, 1936.

Hensley, Herbert C., "Memoirs," unpublished, 1949–1951, Research Archives San Diego Historical Society.

Higgins, Shelley J., This Fantastic City, City of San Diego, San Diego, 1956.

Interviews by the author with Gerald MacMullen, former police reporter and historian.

Interviews by the author with many police officers and members of their families, including five police chiefs from Elmer Jansen to William Kolender; others: David Allsbrook, Jr., Louis Schnug, Jack Golden, Ed Dieckmann, Carroll West, Walter R. Scott, George Churchman, Hugh Rochefort, Robert P. Newsom, Jr., Robert Karrow, James H. Harrell, and John T. Holt.

Jansen, A. E., "Keno Wilson, A Lawman's Lawman," San Diego Historical Quarterly, October 1961.

McGrew, Clarence Alan, San Diego and San Diego County, vols. 1 and 2, American Historical Society, 1922.

Pourade, Richard F., The Glory Years, 1964; Gold in the Sun, 1965; The Rising Tide, 1967; and City of the Dream, 1977. Union-Tribune Publishing Co., San Diego.

Records, Record Bureau of the San Diego Police Department. Microfilm made in the early 1950s of earlier papers, which were then discarded. Only one or two reports on the IWW troubles in 1912 were preserved. Other reports may have been expunged earlier, when the police actions were being investigated by a federal grand jury convened in Los Angeles in 1912 and when investigations of possible civil rights violations were ordered by Gov. Hiram Johnson of California and President William Howard Taft. Few records were saved for the entire period from 1889 to 1930. There appears to have been a desire to destroy documents.

Report on the City Manager Form of Government in San Diego, California, by the Public Administration Services, Chicago, 1939. A pamphlet covering the years 1931–1939.

San Diego Evening Tribune, 1895–1989.

San Diego Sun, 1881–1939.

San Diego Union, 1868–1989.

Smith, Walter G., The Story of San Diego, City Printing Company, 1892.

Smythe, William E., History of San Diego, 1542–1908, The History Company, San Diego, 1908.

Stewart, Don M., Frontier Port, Ward Ritchie Press, Los Angeles, 1965.

Weinstock, Harris, "Disturbances in the City of San Diego and the County of San Diego, California, Report to His Excellency, Hiram W. Johnson, Governor of California," Sacramento, 1912.

The most complete collection extant of San Diego police badges is housed today in an exhibit case in the office of the Chief of Police.

ACKNOWLEDGMENTS

This history is the work of many persons, all of whom had a common purpose in aiding the author—to preserve the heritage of the department.

The Union-Tribune Publishing Company's librarians were most helpful—Charlotte Porte and later Sharon Reeves and their staff. Contributing to the collection of photographs were Charles Sick, director of photography of the U-T, and Raymond Chariker, library assistant in the photo library.

At the San Diego Historical Society, I owe a debt of gratitude to James Moss, who was executive director when this project was launched; Sylvia Arden, head of the library and manuscript collection; Larry and Jane Booth of the photograph collections; Thomas L. Scharf, managing editor of publications; Ann Kantor, associate director; and Richard Crawford, archivist/historian.

Rhoda Kruse, librarian in charge of the San Diego Public Library's California Room, was most helpful.

I owe much to Sgt. Jerry Meloche, retired, for years editor of *Fall In*, a publication of the San Diego Police Officers Association. Also thanks to Bud McKanna, lecturer/historian at San Diego State University; Eric Poulson for helping restore early photographs; and Howard Welty and Ralph Bennett for their editing of the manuscript.

Many, many persons who are or were active in the Police Department deserve credit, particularly Lieutenant John Morrison, the late Clyde Leech, Sergeant Leon Tipton, Marian L. Rogers, Bill Robinson, Bob Lampert, Sergeant Bob Kilpatrick, Lieutenant Les Ginn, Sergeant Bob Jones, the late Sergeant Robert Ristau, Kenneth Sawyer, and Bill Mockler.

Others who contributed generously were Amy Fike, archivist of the City Clerk's office; Marian Brisette, in charge of the archives at the County Law Library; Lori Davisson, research specialist of the Arizona Heritage Center in Tucson; Nancy S. Kinney, director of research, Western Costume Company of Los Angeles; and Neil K. Basen, professor of history, University of Wisconsin, Madison.

And lastly, let me express my gratitude to my wife Barbara for her fifteen years of tolerance.

For any errors of fact or interpretation, the author takes sole responsibility.

INDEX

⬡

BIOGRAPHICAL NOTE

★

Pliny Castanien served as police reporter for the *San Diego Union* for almost twenty-six years. A native of Oklahoma, he attended Oklahoma State and Wichita State and is a World War II veteran. Castanien started his career as a cub reporter for the *Wichita Beacon* in 1931 and was also on the editorial staffs of the *Wichita Evening Eagle* and the *Tulsa Daily World*. He is a member of the Society of Professional Journalists (Sigma Delta Chi), the San Diego Press Club, and the San Diego Historical Society.